# Reflections

edited by

MARILYN MARQUIS **and** SARAH NIELSEN

One World
Many Voices
a collection of student essays

One World Many Voices: Reflections
Copyright © 2011 by Marilyn Marquis and Sarah Nielsen

Published in the United States and the United Kingdom
by WingSpan Press, Livermore, CA

The WingSpan name, logo and colophon are the trademarks of WingSpan Publishing.

ISBN 978-1-59594-415-3

First edition 2010

Printed in the United States of America

www.wingspanpress.com

Library of Congress Control Number 2011921664

1 2 3 4 5 6 7 8 9 10

This collection of essays, *Reflections*, is the fifth book in *One World Many Voices*, a series of collected essays written by and for English language learners. The series stems from an effort to provide easy and interesting extensive reading material for students in the ESL program at Las Positas College, in Livermore, California.

The editors of this series initiated READERS WRITING FOR READERS in 2006 to encourage students to write on a particular topic for readers who are learning English. By participating in READERS WRITING FOR READERS and reading the resulting books, students have the powerful experience of learning from peers and of helping others with their language development. Knowledge comes from students themselves. In reading the writing of their peers, students may simultaneously join a community of readers, discover themselves in the experiences of others, and expand their understanding of the world.

These student-generated essays, edited to control the variety of sentence structure and the range of vocabulary, provide advanced level students with interesting, easy to read and understand material that they can read successfully without the use of a dictionary.

We wish to extend our thanks to the ESL faculty at Las Positas College for engaging their students in READERS WRITING FOR READERS. We are deeply grateful to the students for their genuine and creative contributions.

*Marilyn Marquis and Sarah Nielsen, editors*

# Acknowledgements

WE ARE INDEBTED TO THE students in the English as a second language program at Las Positas College for their enthusiastic participation in READERS WRITING FOR READERS. Their heartfelt writing about their lives, their feelings, their families, their customs, and their struggles with living in a new country has inspired us to create this series of student-generated essays for their extensive reading.

We also want to acknowledge many others who have contributed to this series. Fredda Cassidy and the faculty and students in the Visual Communications program at Las Positas College worked patiently with us to establish the look and feel of these books. They designed the layout, logo, and covers through a truly collaborative process, in particular Linda Roberts, Rebecca Schoefer, Melinda Bandler, and Meg Epperly. Thank you!

Thank you also to the instructors in the English as a Second Language program at Las Positas College for inviting us into their classrooms to present READERS WRITING FOR READERS to their students and for encouraging their students to participate in the project.

We would like to acknowledge the contributions of individuals who offered feedback, suggestions, proofreading, and support, with special thanks to Dr. Philip Manwell, Dean of Arts and Communications at Las Positas College.

# Table of
# Contents

# Remember Me

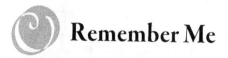

# Remember Me

## A Friend Forever

JOSÉ TORRES

IN THIS LIFE, EACH OF us acts in good and bad ways, but the majority of the time, we are remembered for our good actions rather than our bad ones. Recording artists will be remembered for their greatest hits. Teachers will be remembered for their good qualities such as passion and honesty. My best friend Eduardo would like to be remembered as the best doctor in his area and as an all around nice person. Sometimes I have asked myself how I want to be remembered. I am sure I would like to be remembered by my family and friends for my good actions and positive characteristics. I hope the people who know me can describe me as an honest, friendly, and helpful person because I think these are some of the most important characteristics that every person should develop.

I hope my friends and family will remember my honesty

first and foremost. An honest person is someone who tells the truth and acts on those beliefs, even when it is not an easy thing to do. My parents taught me the importance of honesty when I was a child. They explained that honest people always have honest friends close to them. A perfect example of honest people finding each other happened a few years ago when I found a laptop computer at my school, and I immediately thought about how to return it to its owner. I walked a few feet carrying the computer and noticed many flyers posted in the halls. One flyer said: If you find a laptop, please call and you will be rewarded. Right away I made the phone call, and I met the guy who had lost his laptop a few hours later. He appreciated my honesty so much that he tried to give me a reward. But without hesitating, I told him, "No thank you. Don't worry because it is a pleasure, my friend." Since that day, we have been good friends because he discovered in me a great person with a great quality. Another example of my honesty happened a couple of months ago at work when I found a wad of money without any identification attached. I immediately gave the money to my manager. A few hours later, a gentleman came to reclaim the money, and he gave me a fifty-dollar reward for my honesty. My manager also gave me the day off as a reward to returning the money without touching a single dollar.

In addition to being remembered for my honesty, I would like to be remembered as a friendly person. Being friendly is a good characteristic that many people have naturally. This quality is very important in my own life because it has helped me to make a lot of friends especially at school. I am lucky to have friends from many different countries, and they know that I am with them in the best and worst times. I first met many of these good friends by reaching out and being friendly to people I didn't know. In fact, I always try to make new friends everywhere I go whether I am grabbing a quick bite in a restaurant or waiting for my school bus. Sometimes I find myself striking up a conversation with someone I just met, and after a few minutes, we are talking as if we had been friends for months or even years. My friend Kanani is someone I met a couple of years ago while we were both waiting for the bus. After a short conversation, we discovered that we had many goals in common and have been friends ever since. My friend Beth is another example. We met in line at the bank. Because of her beauty and sweetness, she is the type of woman who cannot be ignored. Our chat at the bank led to coffee and conversation. Now we communicate regularly with each other, and now, happily, she is my best friend.

I would like to be remembered not only as an honest, friendly person, but also as a helpful person. It is important to help others because someday we may need their help ourselves. I believe helpfulness is my strongest quality, one that I have demonstrated in my actions towards others. For example, a long time ago in my hometown there was an earthquake. After the quake, many people had no clothes to wear, no food to eat, and no place to rest at night. My family was fortunate not to be in that situation, so I decided to walk around and look for people who needed help. I found a mother and two children. The mother was crying in the middle of the street, a scared child at each hand. I approached her and asked, "Why are you crying?" She responded, "Because I have no food for my children and no place to sleep tonight." I invited them to my house where my mother and I fed them and let them stay with us for two weeks. Until this day, we have kept a good relationship with them, and they are grateful to my mother and me. Lending a helping hand made me feel quite proud and more aware of how lucky I have been in my life. A similar situation presented itself with my friend Rodrigo. I met him when he asked me for directions late one evening. He was looking for a cheap place to rent because he had just moved from his small town to our city. Given the lateness of the hour, I suggested that he stay with my family that night and look for a place the next day. After a good night's sleep, Rodrigo woke up and soon accepted an offer from us to rent a room in our house for a very cheap price. He still rents a room in my family's home, and we have built a good relationship. I think I won another friend by being helpful one night.

While I am here and after I am gone, I hope my friends and family will remember my good actions and my positive characteristics.

## I Have a Calling

OLGA KNKADE

*I* BELIEVE THAT EVERY TREE CAN speak, and every flower, leaf, stone, grain of sand, and even the Earth, if you would like to listen and communicate. Everything in the world has a spirit, thoughts, its own history, family, and dreams. This is my world, and the purpose of my life is to share it with people, some of whom I hope will remember me.

I created my world when I was a child. Back then I had a lot of friends. The best of all of them was my dog, Pirat, who was like a shadow following me everywhere, who understood me from his very first glance. Other friends lived nearby: apple, cherry, and apricot trees; whole fields of wild flowers;

boundless quantities of bees, bugs, spiders, and butterflies. I watched my friends every day, talked to them, and from the rustle of their leaves, from the buzzing of their wings, from the silence of their thoughts, I could guess what they were saying back to me.

Crouched under trees or lying on grass, I loved reading books to those friends who listened to me attentively. I was a very innocent child, and I accepted all the stories that I read about adventures or incredible heroes as absolute, undeniable truth. Books helped to invigorate my imagination, and I started creating my own stories. Two fighting bugs, for instance, were not just bugs in my eyes. I would name them, relate them to one of the bug families, and describe their fighting as qualifying events for the Olympics. Each of them would have a favorite food, a beloved song, and maybe even a secret girlfriend. I loved creating my stories and couldn't live without them. Whenever a picture I had seen captured my interest, I immediately drew a story in my mind.

In my heart, I am the same as I was 20 years ago and still believe that a full life exists in everything. I now wish to connect my world to other people. I believe my love for writing and making art is how I can express myself and make that connection. I would like my works to lead to changes in people's attitude towards Nature. Through my books and pictures, I hope to help people understand how sensitive Nature is and how she needs our love and care, especially now when Nature is not just in need, but in crisis. My goal, however, is not to point attention to what we have done. I intend to encourage people to make changes.

In my writing, I will work on literature for young readers who are just forming their perceptions and values about the world and its inhabitants. Through engrossing stories with subtexts, I will entertain them, and at the same time, teach them how our world is alive and needs our love. My ideas for artwork are the same as for my writing, but they will be through representation in painting and mostly for adult audiences.

I can hear the whispering of Nature, what she would love me to do with my abilities. I believe my mission is to bring very important, though obvious, information to people's minds through my stories and artwork, and this is how I want to be remembered.

## My Future Self
TAK

*I* HOPE TO BE KNOWN AS a challenger, someone who tries many things that other people normally would not. It doesn't matter that some of the things I try might get thrown away or not get completed at all. This may seem counter-intuitive, but let me explain.

Getting things started is very important. For instance, even though I know a lot of people in Japan who are eager to study abroad to improve their English skills, not many actually realize that desire. Most of them will find any excuse for not working on their dream. I asked a friend why, and he explained, "I wish I could, but it's been busy at work lately, and I have to study English hard in Japan first, and..." If he really had wanted to study abroad, he'd have already gone to live in some English-speaking country. Regardless of how well things go it is best to try. If my friend lived abroad and became a fluent English speaker, he might not have landed a better a job. He might think: what a waste of time it was to spend all those years away from home. But those experiences abroad—meeting many people from all over the world, adapting to a totally different way of living—could affect his later life in important ways.

One of my dreams is to start a business. Because I believe that entrepreneurs need a tremendous amount of experience to be successful, I seek out unknown and unfamiliar experiences wherever and whenever I can. In a large company, there are various departments such as sales, general accounting, and personnel management. An entrepreneur, on the other hand, has to cover all those departments and more. He inevitably needs more experiences than other people for the times when he might confront difficulties. I myself use every opportunity, even the tiniest one, to gain more experience. I never go home the same way, for example, and if I see an interesting place, I'll drop in. I might stop at a café for coffee and ice cream or join a jam session at a bar. (Did I mention I've played drums for a couple of years?) Stopping in someplace new I might meet somebody who could be my future business partner. In fact, one time I met a middle-aged woman this way who later invited me to join her band. Thanks to her I have the opportunity to be on stage every other Wednesday. Though this is a musical rather than business relationship, meeting her is an important piece of my entire life.

I honestly don't know how these kinds of experiences will affect my life later. These aren't the experiences of gaining technical skills in architecture or biology like a student at a university might have. But this time living in the USA will make my future an active and engaged one; no matter what kind of job I take. Since none of us can restart our lives, at the end of my life, I want to say, "There is nothing I missed in my life."

# The Small Things
## GUADALUPE WHEELER

TALKING ABOUT DEATH IS VERY uncomfortable, especially when we have to talk about our own future death. Sometimes talking about death can be frightening and even cause us to get chills; however, inevitably, every single human being will suffer death whether we like it or not. When I was a child, the subject of someone's death used to scare me to the point that I believed that the dead person would appear at night, dragging me out of my bed and taking me through the window and into the darkness. I thought if I misbehaved or cursed, the dead from the cemetery would come looking for me. I remember from a young age hearing scary stories about this happening to young children who misbehaved or did not listen to their parents. As I grew older, I came to realize that these were only stories meant to scare children into behaving and listening to their parents.

Growing up in Mexico and attending many funerals with my mother was not one of the easiest things for a kid. Most of the time, I looked with curiosity at the deceased person. He or she looked pale and smelled disgusting. At that time, it was rare for a person to be embalmed, especially if they were from a small poor town. When I tried to sleep at night, I would remember the dead person and have nightmares. In those reoccurring dreams, I either struggled to see the person inside the casket but could not, or I chose to stay away, against the expectations of my culture.

My point of view about death has radically changed through the years. As years passed and I matured, I learned to cope with the loss of loved ones and learned to be strong. Living outside my native country, Mexico, and reading books including the Bible have helped me learn to face death differently. Now I believe the dead are resting, waiting for God's judgment. Due to my faith, I can accept my own death more freely and not be fearful of it. This also helps me deal with death in general because I know my loved ones will die someday.

My response to suffering has also changed. The fact that people abuse their power or authority makes me angry and motivates me to care for the less fortunate. My father had surgery twice, and I spent many nights taking care of him since it was too difficult for my mother. In addition, my older brother spent almost a year in the hospital because of five brain surgeries, and I tried to help as much as possible at home, since he was like a baby for a couple of months. One of my older sisters had a baby in January this year in Las Vegas, and I went to help her with her children for a week. Another sister, who lives in London, had a baby this past May, and I travelled across the Atlantic to spend a month with her.

I have witnessed my mother and siblings caring for each other as well as helping people around us. This is the greatest example that leads me to do as well as I possibly can in this life. I have tried to be kind, helpful and caring to my family, my friends, the elderly, children, and animals, which are innocent, susceptible and inoffensive creatures. In fact, helping homeless children in Mexico as well as the elderly and animals are causes that I am proud to say that I have contributed to in some way. There are innocent people around the world who need protection, food, and shelter. I have good feelings as well as good intentions when it comes to helping the less fortunate. I believe that we can do something about their needs and encourage others to follow in our footsteps. These seemingly small actions are important in our individual lives and can make a difference in the wider world.

My moral values were learned in my family by example, through acts of love, devotion, patience, kindness, and compassion. More important than my family's teachings, however, is what I choose to follow and practice based on those teachings. Helping without expecting anything in return and the satisfaction that I did it are enough to keep in my heart forever. In the end, I am not going to take anything with me. The only things that last in people's hearts are those little things, those small gestures that transform their lives. My desires and hopes are that this kind of thinking and action will grow rapidly, rippling out widely and changing the world. This is how I would like to be remembered.

## Leaving Cuba
YURISLADY RODRIGUEZ

IN THE HISTORY OF THE world, there are countless human feats that have been documented. Some people are remembered and admired for courageous acts or brilliant ideas, which changed human history in some way. Others, though not famous, still leave an important mark on the world, and people who knew them think about them after they are gone. Someone will remember each of us in some way.

Living in this world has always been complicated. At some point or another, each of us will face difficulties in our lives. In today's world, there are many people who have overcome obstacles in order to reach their goals and make their lives easier. We as human beings make decisions in our daily lives that can be remembered in different ways.

I still have in my mind those scary and sad days when I was planning to leave my beautiful island of Cuba in order to study English in London. It was absolutely the hardest decision I have ever made in my entire life because I knew I was going to a whole new world where everything and everyone was going to be different from what I had known before. Arriving alone in a new country, learning a new language, meeting new people would be a real challenge, I knew. Not long after I left my country, I realized more fully how truly new and different the world was outside of Cuba. After experiencing the privileges I enjoyed in England and gaining knowledge about how my life could be, I decided not to return to my unforgettable island.

My decision to stay in London and later move to the United States definitely surprised a lot of people including my family and friends. Some friends and family members spread horrible rumors about why I had not returned to Cuba and how I had left behind the ones who truly cared about me. Others were absolutely excited and happy that I had made such a huge decision and could see the long-term benefits this decision could bring for my family. In all the positive and negative comments I received about my decision, my mother's voice was the most worried, afraid and concerned. At first, she thought I had made the most unintelligent decision in my entire life. However, after a few months when she realized I was interested in continuing my studies and working toward a better future in the United States, she changed her mind completely. It was then when my lovely and beautiful mom started to recognize the purpose behind my decision. Now every time we talk on the phone, she tells me in her angelic voice how proud she is of me and how much she admires and values everything I have accomplished so far.

Thinking beyond my professional future and all the goals I have for my life, I also think about the day I will have a beautiful family. I believe everyone wants to be remembered as an excellent parent who fought hard to protect his or her family. In fact, one of the important factors in my decision to stay here was the benefit to my future children. I still remember my childhood without a doll or any other toy. I longed for a bicycle, but never got one. Because of my family's poor economic position, my mother and father could not afford to buy my brother or me those things we longed for. I hope one day that my own children will understand why I came here and appreciate the sacrifices I made for their future. I definitely want my family to remember me as a person who wasn't ever afraid of doing anything in life as long as it would benefit the family.

## Memories of Me

JOSÉ A. ANGELES

MANY PEOPLE WANT TO BE remembered because of all that they accumulated in their lives, but for me, it is more important to be remembered for what I did best. I want to be remembered for my actions, not for empty words or meaningless objects. When I am gone from this world, I want to be remembered positively, especially by my wife, my kids, and my future grand kids. When I think about the memories my family will have about me, it makes me work very hard in life because I want them to appreciate all the good things that I have done and will do for them.

I want my kids to remember me as a good father who taught them well the lessons of life. I want them to value my efforts to move to another country in order to provide them with a good education and a better life. I moved to the USA knowing this country could give me a lot of great opportunities. Moving here was really difficult, though, because I had to learn to speak a new language and get used to the people and customs of this new country. After I moved to the USA, I started to sacrifice everything because I wanted my family to have financial security. For example, although I enjoy dancing and going to parties, I have sacrificed my enjoyment in order to work more and save money for my family. I am not only working hard for our future, I am also studying hard to get a good education and find a better job. Right now I have an important goal to accomplish, which is to become a professional web designer. This goal is important to me because I know I will make good money and support my family well. I hope my children and the rest of my family will value and appreciate my hard work and my academic pursuits. I hope also that they will follow my example as they build their own lives.

I also want to be remembered as a person who was kind and giving to others. I am always thinking about and doing things for other people. For example, I have helped every December by giving away free food and gifts to poor people. I want to keep doing this until I die. In my opinion, helping others is really important because you never know when you are going to need some help yourself. I really want people to value my efforts to reach out and help others. Before I die, I plan to donate money to help all those people who don't have a place to live and hope that others will be inspired to follow in my footsteps.

In short, I want to be remembered for the great things that I did for my family and for other people. I don't want to be remembered for looking beautiful or for having many material possessions. I want all my accomplishments to be of great value to the people who appreciated my actions and remember me for those actions. I am hopeful that my dream will come true one day.

CHAPTER TWO

# Beginnings

The Miracle of Birth

Korean Traditions

A Baby's Birth

Chinese Traditions

In Indonesia

Seven-Month Ritual

Born in Ukraine

 **Beginnings**

## The Miracle of Birth

OLGA SPASIBENKO

*G*IVING BIRTH IS A MIRACLE that human females are granted by nature. A woman has the privilege of feeling a baby develop in her stomach as mother and baby live together bodily for nine long months. For me, my pregnancy was one of the best periods in my life. An especially high point was when the fetus started to move for the first time. I was sitting at work and suddenly felt a push from inside. I had not understood the significance of life within me before that happened. But when I realized what happened, I was filled with joy and my face lit up with a shinning smile. I suffered waiting to the end of the workday so I could see my husband and tell him what had just happened and hope that he, too, could feel these light pushes.

In Russia, a woman can stop working and take maternity leave when she is seven months pregnant. For the next two months, she can completely devote herself to her pregnancy and prepare for the arrival of the new baby. In the past, before the middle of the twentieth century, there was a tradition to not buy clothes and other baby things until after the baby's birth. Now, most people don't follow this tradition. They usually have a nursery ready for the new baby. There are still, however, no baby showers in Russia prior to the birth. After two months of preparation, the new parents are ready for the arrival of their new baby.

When a woman feels that important moment has come, she goes to hospital. There are two kinds of maternity hospitals: public and private. The public hospital has one big advantage and one big disadvantage over the private hospital. At a public hospital, the delivery is almost free, but the husband cannot be present. I gave birth to my daughter, Sofia, in such a public maternity hospital eight years ago early one winter morning. I regret that my husband could not attend the delivery; I think it would have been a big help to me. After the delivery, I was very tired, so the doctor encouraged me to rest alone for two hours. After that, I had a chance to see my little daughter and breast feed for the first time, which was an indescribable experience. I remember making eye contact with my daughter during feeding and only at that moment did I understand how I was the whole universe for my baby. I would like to have shared these early experiences with my husband.

My husband came to the hospital a little later, but he couldn't come in my room, so I had to show him our little daughter through the window. I remember his tearful happy eyes and his thumbs up signal, meaning *cool baby*. While mother and baby remained at the hospital, the new father was arranging a party. He invited his friends to celebrate the day of our baby's birth with him. Sofia and I stayed at the hospital for five days, which is the typical time to remain confined. On the fifth day, my husband brought us home.

In Russia, women can stay home from work to take care of a baby for one and a half years. She can devote all of her time to ensuring the health and happiness of the child. I appreciated that time. Traditionally, parents waited a month to invite family and friends to become acquainted with the new baby. This gives the parents time to relax with their new son or daughter and gives the baby time to adjust.

There are some special celebrations during the first year, but one of the most significant is the christening. Some people do it only because it is a tradition. Some don't follow this tradition at all, but most parents christen their children to invite God's protection. Our daughter was christened when she was a year and a half old. She has a godfather and a godmother who have promised to love and protect her and to encourage her spiritual life. She still wears the cross that was given to her by the priest at the end of the christening ceremony.

## Korean Traditions

ANONYMOUS

WHEN I WAS A LITTLE girl, I heard about some traditional birth customs that are unique to Korea. Koreans have always done things according to custom and with great politeness, so they have many long standing customs regarding the birth of a child.

First of all, in the past there were many restrictions placed on the expectant mother. For example, she had to isolate herself from the outside world. She could not go outside for any reason especially for the twenty-one days before giving birth. During this confinement, the only person she could meet with was her mother. Not even her neighbors could see her. She also could not take a shower, even if the weather was very hot. This was a typical approach to maternity protection for twenty-one days. When I was pregnant my mother told me not to follow this tradition because when she followed it, she had skin problems. She told me the unfortunate but amusing story about her pregnancy, which made me laugh then and still makes me laugh when I think of it.

Another unique Korean birth custom is hanging up a leaf in front of the door. Ancient Korean's believed that the leaf could prevent suffering evil or bad luck, and it could keep away illness. Also according to tradition, if the parents hoped for a boy, they hung red peppers or pine twigs on the fence around the house. If they hoped for a girl, they hung up a piece of charcoal. These two very different items symbolize Korean attitudes about girls and boys. The capsicum or red chili peppers symbolize incantation or enchantment. Red is an important color in Korean culture. In contrast, the charcoal symbolized impurities and the need to cleanse the impurities before the birth.

Korea also has some traditions about the day a baby is born. A very lucky day to be born is August Fifteenth. This is liberation or Independence Day in Korea. An unlucky day to be born is June 6 because this is Memorial Day in Korea, a day when we celebrate the lives of the deceased.

Learning about these special customs helps us to understand the lessons of our ancestors. We should pass the knowledge of traditional customs to our children even though most women will not follow them.

# A Baby's Birth
### ANONYMOUS

MEXICO HAS MANY DIFFERENT CUSTOMS related to preparing for a new baby's birth. Some of the customs are regional and some are common to the whole culture. Some customs concern the restrictions on the pregnant mother and others concern the ways we welcome the new baby into our lives. In every part of the country, children are seen as a blessing on the family.

In the region where I came from, a pregnant woman must take particular care. For example, she cannot color her hair, cannot drink tea, cannot paint her fingernails, and cannot take any kind of medicine for fear that these things could damage the baby. Also during the pregnancy, friends of the parents hold a little party for the new mom, and the friends who attend this celebration bring some presents for the future baby. They also make predictions about the gender of the new baby. Most people believe that if the pregnant woman has a round belly, the baby will be a girl, but if the belly goes up and out, the baby will be a boy. If the parents already know the gender of the baby, people will buy appropriate presents for a boy or a girl. During the party, people talk about having a baby and help the parents get ready for the big event.

Before the baby is born the husband usually makes some preparations. He gets a video camera to record the baby's birth so that he can be in the hospital and capture the birth on video. Then, the parents keep this video as a valuable treasure. In addition, if the baby is a boy, the husband gives a cigar to his family and close friends. If the baby is a girl, he gives marshmallows. I am not sure what these things represent, but most new dads follow this tradition.

We have some interesting ideas about how to take care of the baby during the early months after delivery. When the mother and baby first come home from the hospital, they stay alone together for several days. After this time, the relatives can come to visit the new member of the family. People also believe that you should not, even gently, shake the baby because his or her cheeks will fall down. Also, the mother should not face the baby backward because the baby might become cross-eyed. Finally, the parents should not allow anyone to cut the baby's hair because this could cause the baby to not talk well.

These traditions are important in my family because this is the way that my brothers, sisters, and I grew up. Generation after generation, we have kept these traditions when someone has a baby. I hope to continue these same customs in the USA. If I marry someone from my own culture, it will be easy, but if I marry a lady from a different culture with different customs, we will choose the best customs for us and have a successful married relationship.

## Chinese Traditions
YAN YANG

A BABY'S BIRTH BRINGS GREAT HAPPINESS to a family. During the first year, the rapid mental and physical development is celebrated with joy and importance in Chinese culture. Family and friends share the experiences of the baby's first year with several important celebrations.

Several days after the baby is born, the family announces the birth with a special event. As an announcement to the whole village that the family has a newborn, the father visits the neighbors and friends to deliver symbolic gifts. If the baby is a boy, the family prepares dyed red eggs. If the baby is a girl, the family prepares sticky rice cakes. These two foods symbolize our hope for good luck and peace. During older times, eggs and rice were two very nutritious and precious foods. Since a newborn is believed to bring the family good lucky and peace, we want to share those nutritious good foods to symbolize sharing our joyful moment with relatives, friends, and neighbors.

One month after the birth, most families invite relatives and important friends to a party. At the party, all of the guests will present lucky money or gold to the baby. The gifts are sealed in a vivid red envelope or box. During the party, guests are served the best foods and wine. This party welcomes the new baby into the community of family and friends.

Another celebration, which happens at home, is shaving the baby's hair and using it to make a writing brush. There are two reasons for this event. First, we believed that a baby's hair grows back thicker after it is shaved. Second, the parents want to have a souvenir writing brush made from the baby's hair. This writing brush seals the pleasant memories for years. Later the brush is a gift to the young adult. Unfortunately, it's difficult to have this kind of ceremony in the United States, but it is still important, so I collected some of my baby's hair as it fell out and saved it in an envelope. Some day I hope to make a writing brush as a gift for a special occasion.

Another important event is celebrated when the baby is one hundred days old. In addition to the numbers six and eight, one hundred symbolizes good luck and a long and fulfilled life. There is not necessarily a party on that day, but the parents record the baby's physical development. Most parents also have the baby's portrait taken to commemorate one hundred days. Some families shave the baby's hair on that day if they didn't do it when the baby was one month old.

The end of the first year is always very important. Most families have a first birthday party with family and friends. The most fun part of that day is watching the baby choose a career. The parents pick twelve items; each one symbolizes a different career. The baby will pick one item among the twelve to reveal his or her future career. This activity stems from old superstitions. At one time, people might have believed that the item indicated the baby's real future career or character. Of course, there is no scientific proof for these results. Now we enjoy the activity for fun and good wishes. The items also reveal something about the parents' hopes for their baby. The following twelve items are frequently selected:

- An abacus suggests strong logic thinking.
- A book relates to teaching or researching.
- A coin suggests a career in finance.
- A pen relates to publishing.
- A seal relates to political power.
- A sword suggests a career related to the military or law enforcement.
- A globe of the earth relates to agriculture or horticulture.
- A ruler means a career related to design.
- Meat suggests a career in cooking or service.
- Celery indicates that the baby will be diligent.
- An orange indicates that the baby will be very lucky.
- A green onion indicates that the baby will be smart and good at socializing.

We carried out this activity for our baby here in the United States, too. We put those twelve items in a big circle on the floor. I remembered her crawling on the floor and playing with almost everything. In the end, she was absorbed in playing with a soft sewing ruler. She entwined herself in it and could not get herself out. We were all amused. I don't seriously believe that her choice predicts her future. I believe, however, that carrying out the traditional activities reveals our best wishes for her future.

We are first generation immigrants to the United States, so we don't have relatives here. It has been difficult to have the traditional Chinese celebrations for our daughter without our families, but we have new friends to celebrate with now. Even though we have missed celebrating with our families, we cherish our first year of parenting.

## In Indonesia
### LINDA KHO

I CAME FROM INDONESIA, WHICH IS thought of as a conservative country, especially in contrast to the United States. Indonesia also has many different cultures and each one has its own traditions. As a Chinese-Indonesian, we have our own special cultures and traditions, which are quite different from the local Indonesian traditions. Many Chinese-Indonesians still follow some of the Chinese traditions for pregnancy and naming children.

For example, we have some rules or superstitions from the elders that a pregnant woman has to obey. Even though people nowadays don't really believe in those superstitions anymore, we think it's better to listen to our elders than to have regrets in the future. For example, during the pregnancy, members of the family have some restrictions.

They are not supposed to move furniture in the house as it will affect the fetus, and the woman might miscarry. Painting the house can cause the baby to be born with spots the same color as the house on parts of its body or sometimes on its face. Cutting things on the bed is believed to cause the baby to be born with a handicap or cleft pallet. I often heard stories that confirm these beliefs, but most people do not really believe them. One additional superstition is that after a woman has given birth, she has to stay out of the shower and can't even wash her hair for a month! I really doubt anyone can tolerate that now.

In my family, we don't have a baby shower before the baby is born. During the first few days after the birth, some relatives and the mother's friends come to visit and bring a gift or a red packet, which contains some money to offer their blessings to the baby. When the baby is a full month old, the baby has its hair shaved, and the family gives boxes of cake to relatives and friends. After that, the relatives and friends who received the cake will bring gifts for the baby in return. Of course, those who have given a gift before don't have to do that again. On that day, the baby is brought to the maternal grandparents' house for a gathering, which is very important in my culture because it's our way of letting people know about the birth of our new family member so the baby can receive their blessings. It also brings joy and creates a chance for the whole family to gather together.

In another tradition, we all have two names given by our parents, an Indonesian name and a Chinese name. In my family, our Indonesian names are chosen by our parents and do not have to be followed by any family name because we don't have any. In other words, these names are optional for those who have family names. As for the Chinese name, it usually consists of three Chinese characters, but some people have only two characters, which is fine. With either three or sometimes two characters, the first character must be the family name. For Chinese-Indonesians, having a Chinese name is important because it identifies us as Chinese and reminds us where our ancestors came from. As Buddhists, we also have religious names given after we are formally acknowledged and receive the blessing from a monk. But most people don't use these as their formal names.

In a Chinese family, usually they would have a book of family names, and it's usually used for naming the male descendants because male descendants, who are considered very important, carry on the family-line. I think this part of Chinese tradition is unfair because most people also pass on their wealth or property to their eldest male descendant in the family while females don't receive anything. Fortunately, this custom is changing, and some people don't do what people in the past used to do. Now some people pass their wealth on to any descendants that they would like to give it to.

Now, in a totally new country, with new people, new cultures, new challenges, and new environment, we don't think that we will continue those traditions anymore. As members of the younger generation, those traditions are not suitable for us, but we will still remember them.

# Seven-Month Ritual

RATU BUCHANAN

INDONESIA IS MADE UP OF many islands, regions, and cultures, all of which celebrate a woman's pregnancy differently. My family is from the island of Sumatra, and we have very unique celebrations when a woman reaches the seventh month of her pregnancy. The rituals, *Nujuh Bulanan*, *Slametan*, and *Mitoni*, demonstrate gratitude for surviving danger or bad luck. These are a way of asking for divine blessings. The *Mitoni* ritual was especially important for me. In my family, we firmly believe that a seven-month old fetus possesses a soul and that the life should be protected and celebrated. This is especially important for the first pregnancy, since the first child is said to bring good luck to the family and the later siblings.

Like other traditional ceremonies, *Mitoni* is practiced in different fashions in different regions. Mine started with a *kenduri*, a ritual gathering with meals and religious prayers. My family and my neighbors all attended my first *Mitoni*, which was guided by the village elders who gave me a bathing ritual with water from seven wells, my own and six of my neighbors. This symbolized that my baby, upon birth, would be blessed by my family as well as by our neighbors. After the bathing, I was offered two yellow coconuts; they were split and I drank part of the milk from each one in the hope that the good characters of *Arjuna* and *Sumbadra*, Hindu goddesses, would be absorbed by my infant's soul. Virtue and serenity are what this ceremony is all about. The goddess, *Arjuna*, symbolizes that if I bear a boy, he will be handsome and chivalrous. The goddess *Sumbadra*, princess, symbolizes that if I bear a girl, she will be beautiful and faithful like *Sumbadra*.

In addition to the two young yellow coconuts, two ivory coconuts were carved with images of two Gods. One has an image of the God, *Kamajaya*, the handsome and faithful God, and one has the Goddess *Ratih*, the beautiful and faithful Goddess. These two coconut carvings symbolize the hope that the baby will be born safely and that a baby boy will be handsome like *Kamajaya*, and a baby girl will be beautiful like *Ratih*. My husband selected one of the two coconuts without knowing which God's image was carved on it. He cut through it using a sharp knife. Custom requires that if the coconut splits in two, guests say, "It's a girl." If the coconut milk emerges as from a fountain, they say, "It's a boy." Then I carefully carried the coconut in a cloth sling to our bed.

After this we had to perform *Angrem*, which means hatching eggs. For this part of the ritual, my husband and I sat on a pile of Batik cloth as if we were sitting on a nest of eggs so that the baby would be delivered safely and on time. After that, we ate food together from the *Sajen* offering, where the food had been put on a big stone plate called *Cobek*. The traditional *Sajen* offering is an important part of the ritual, so my husband and I had to eat all of the food. For example, we ate *tumpeng*, which is a cone of rice with vegetables and meat around it. We ate seven kinds of *sambal*. *Sambal shich* is a hot, spicy side dish of chili peppers that ensures an active and creative life for our child. *Sabal rujak* is a mixture of fruits and *sambal* sauce. Sweet cookies from peanuts and other traditional cakes from rice and sugar ensure a sweet life. Vegetable side dishes ensure a healthy baby. Red and white porridge are also important. Red porridge ensures that the baby will remember and respect his or her mother, and white porridge symbolizes the same for the father. Fruits with different kinds of cooked rice, like *gurih* rice cooked with coconut milk, *punar ric* rice cooked with tumeric and *kebuli* rice are important parts of the feast. The decorations include dolls, which represent both a boy and a girl and help the parents to welcome either one. In every ritual, we always use every part of a coconut tree because the fruit, the leaves, and the wood are all valuable. This symbolizes our hope that our baby will be a useful human being.

At the end of the ritual, my husband and I served *rujak,* a mixture of sliced fruit and hot *sambal,* and *dawet,* a sweet refreshing drink made of coconut milk mixed with sugar and small pieces of soft rice cookies. The guests exchanged a piece of earthen tile for the drinks. This piece of tile, *rujak,* symbolizes an enthusiastic life. *Dawet* is a healthy drink that we call *dawet plencing*; we serve it to symbolize a smooth and safe birth.

Finally, the ritual was complete after my husband slept all night in the same bed with the second coconut as an exercise for patiently caring for a new baby. In the morning, my husband broke the second coconut, symbolizing our efforts to avoid selfishness and to help and appreciate each other.

## Born in Ukraine

ANONYMOUS

I WAS BORN IN UKRAINE IN 1976. At that time, women delivered babies in a special hospital. Only medical doctors and nurses could be in that hospital with the new mothers and babies. I was five days old when my father first held me and took me home. Today, the father and other close relatives can enter the hospital and stay in the delivery room. However, other Ukrainian customs have not changed as much since I was born.

The first several weeks, the parents do not invite guests to meet the new baby. The new baby stays home with only the mother and father. The parents, in the past, isolated and protected the baby at home for forty days. According to some old superstitions, the baby's soul was not yet with the body, so the parents protected the baby from bad luck or bad spirits. Today, we also keep the baby at home for several weeks, but now we protect the baby from germs and disease.

After those forty days, the parents take the baby to the church for a ceremony where the parents ask for God's protection for the baby. They also give the baby a name. Before the ceremony, the mother cannot eat meat for one week. She prays at home every day and goes to church to confess her sins, and the pastor then asks her to say special prayers. Then they select a date for the church ceremony. The parents ask two special people to be the godmother and godfather. For the ceremony, the godparents, relatives, and friends wear formal clothes to the church, which is decorated with beautiful flowers. During the ceremony, the priest puts a cross on a chain around the baby's neck. The godfather holds the baby and says special prayers as the priest pours water on the baby's head. This ceremony welcomes the baby into the church and protects the baby from bad luck. We also select the baby's name from a special book. The names come from the past and bring good characteristics to the baby.

In Ukraine, we do not have baby showers or give the baby any gifts before the birth because this might bring bad luck to the baby. After forty days, the parents can invite friends and family to a party where they can meet the new baby. Guests usually bring gifts for the baby. Some people bring clothes or baby supplies. Some give family treasures, something from a grandmother or grandfather, and tell the story of these gifts at the party.

Traditions in Ukraine are changing quickly in modern times, so some traditions from my childhood are different from today. Now I live in the USA and my own children will have different traditions.

# Our Names

# Our Names

## Names

HUGO VERA

MOST PEOPLE DO NOT KNOW the way they got their names. In fact, most of them do not even know what their names mean. I know this because I asked my classmates, and almost half of them did not know. I know from having my own children that naming a newborn baby is not easy. I was born in Mexico into a large traditional Mexican family with six boys and four girls. We lived in a small city with a large Catholic influence. In Mexico, there are many ways of giving names to a new baby, but one of those ways and how people celebrate it has been changing.

Parents used to name their children by taking the saint name from a religious calendar. This was a tradition followed by almost every family in the whole country until the middle of the last century. I do not know how or when this tradition started, but since the Spanish conquered

Mexico, and Spain is a Catholic country, it is probable that the saint calendar tradition was acquired as a religious tradition from the Roman Catholic Church when Mexico adopted the Roman Catholic religion. Almost every calendar in Mexico comes with the name of a saint below the date, so a new baby is given the saint's name from the calendar on the day he or she is born. For example, my brother was born on November Eleventh. The saint name on this day is Saint Martin. This is the name given to my older brother by my parents, without the word saint, of course. My mom was born on November Twenty-seventh. The name that appears on that day is Saint Antonieta, so her name in Antonia. The parents can add or subtract some letters to create a girl's name or boy's name accordingly. Many people that I know got their names this way.

There are also two days that the people in Mexico believe are special. Boys who are born into Roman Catholic families on December 25 are named Jesus. These boys are believed to have a special blessing. Girls who are born on December 12 are given the name Maria Guadalupe because this is the feast day of Our Lady of Guadalupe who appeared to children in Mexico. These two days are the most important days for the people in Mexico. I cannot explain exactly why so many women are named Maria, but this is the name of the mother of Jesus, so perhaps parents honor her by giving her name to their daughters.

After the parents name their children, they take them to the church with their godparents to receive a blessing from the priest. This usually happens on Sundays because the majority of the people go to church on this day. This celebration is called Baptism. After this, the parents, relatives, and invited friends go to the family home to celebrate this important event. The parents offer traditional

Mexican drinks and food, such as barbecued lamb, *tortillas, mole*, rice, beans, tequila, and fruit water. This event marks the beginning of a Catholic life.

This tradition of giving children a saint name from the calendar has been changing. Now it is not as common for people to name their children this way. For example, in my family, only my mom and my brother were named this way. I got my name from a famous Mexican soccer player. His name is Hugo Sanchez, so my name is Hugo. I believe that the global influence, the Internet, modern life, and changing attitudes cause parents to name their children without the help of a church calendar. Now, children have very different names.

I know we all got our names in different ways, and we consider our names to be special, but the way the people in Mexico used to give the name to a newborn was exciting and very important.

## Family Names
### JOSÉ TORRES

ONE THING THAT MAKES EACH of us unique is our name because our names give us a special and unique identity. Choosing the right name is not an easy task for parents who always want a beautiful and unique name for their child. Normally parents choose the names of their children, and sometimes they select a name for their new baby before the birth. In Mexico, we have many traditions or ways to choose the names for children, including choosing the father's name, selecting the saint name from the religious calendar, or looking in books with lists of names along with the special meaning of the name.

Many families prefer to give the first child the name of a parent. A boy is given his father's name, and a girl is given her mother's name. This is very traditional in my country. I have many friends who have their father's name as a first name. For example, my father's name is José, and I am sure that my grandfather's name was José; following this tradition, my parents named me José. They are hoping that my first son will be named José. Another example of this tradition is my friend Eduardo whose name comes from his father and his grandfather. His parents and grandparents are also hoping that he will name his first baby boy Eduardo.

Other parents do not choose to name a child after the mother or the father, but instead they find the name on a religious calendar on the day of the baby's birth. For example, my best friend, Ramona, told me that her name comes from the calendar. She was born on August 31, and the calendar shows the name Ramon for a boy and Ramona for a girl. I think Ramona is a lovely name, but not everyone is so fortunate. For example, it is not the case with my friend Inocencia. She always says she has an ugly, weird name. My friend, Inocencia, was born on December 28, which in Mexico is the day of the innocents or of noble descent, so that is why her parents called her Inocencia as shown on the calendar. My cousin Calixto is another example. He always says, "I have an ugly, weird name." His parents called him Calixto because he was born in October 14, and the calendar shows that name. My friends Ramona and Inocencia and my cousin Calixto say that their parents should have chosen other ways to name their children.

In addition to choosing a parent's name or searching the name on the calendar, parents might also choose the names of their children from a book that has the meaning of the names. Some parents decide to look for names in books because they want to find beautiful and unusual names for their babies. For example, my friend Megan's parents found that name in a book. They named her Megan because they found that the name means strong and capable. I think her name shows her real identity because she is a strong and very capable person. Another example of selecting a name from a book comes from my sister's boyfriend, Pedro. His parents chose his name because it means love and friendship. I think he really is a very lovely, nice, friendly person. Finally, my niece Monica has her name because her mom was looking for a beautiful name with a strong meaning. She chose Monica, which means advisor. This choice was perfect for her as she really is a person who offers sound advice to her friends and family.

Choosing a name for a baby is not an easy task for parents who want a beautiful and unique name for their baby. Parents recognize that a name can inspire a child and establish his or her unique character. They consider the name to be part of the personality of each person. Parents have many options for making the choice of a name for their new baby, but each choice comes from the same place, the parents' desire for the perfect name for their new baby.

# Japanese Naming Traditions

MAKI KOGA

PARENTS CHOOSE NAMES FOR THEIR children that reflect their values and tastes. My parents chose my name with consideration for the beauty of the sound of the name as well as for the significance of its meaning. The traits associated with my first name, Maki, have influenced my personality and contributed to my place in the world. Most Japanese parents do not give their children a middle name, so parents select a first name that will have a balance of sound and meaning with the last name.

The Japanese language is unique because it has four writing systems. *Kanji* uses the same characters as Chinese with the Chinese meaning, but the characters also have Japanese meaning and Japanese pronunciation. Each character has a unique meaning, but some pronunciations can be realized with more than one possible *kanji*. This is because Japanese uses almost two thousand different characters in *kanji*. Japanese also has *hiragana*, a writing system that is based only on sounds and is used for Japanese words. Japanese also has *katakana*, which is used for words borrowed from other languages. Finally, Japanese uses the western alphabet to write Japanese words. My name can only be written as Maki using the western alphabet, but using *kanji*, it could have the same pronunciation but have a totally different meaning according to the meaning of the *kanji* characters. Most Japanese names are written in *kanji* for the official name. These Chinese characters describe concepts and have unique meanings.

My name, Maki, was given to me by my grandmother and inspired by her best friend, Maki. The *kanji* means abundant happiness. Maki is one of the most common names in Japan, but the *kanji*, which my parents chose, is very rare. As a matter of fact, I have never met anyone who has the exact same name in *kanji*. My grandmother and my parents loved not only the meaning but also the pronunciation of Maki. Once they decided on my name, my parents took it to a fortune teller, who predicts the child's fortune based on the number of stroke counts in the *kanji* characters. Each character of *kanji* has a particular number of strokes or lines. Simple characters have two or three strokes; more complex characters have six or seven, some even more. These characters combine to make words or names. Names may have two or three characters, each with any number of strokes. The peculiar custom of asking a fortune teller to help select the *kanji* for a child's name still remains popular in Japan; however, it is more popular in modern times to rely on special books for advice on names. My parents chose my name with two *kanji* characters and together there are fifteen strokes, three strokes for Ma and twelve strokes for Ki. So, my particular name is unique in Japanese *kanji*, but in the western alphabet it looks like every other Maki.

I had an interesting experience with my name being confused with a popular type of sushi. About fifteen years ago, my parents invited an American to our house in Japan. When he asked me my name and I told him, Maki, he said that my name sounded just like a type of sushi and wondered if it was related. I was very disappointed and too young to accept or understand this as a joke. Now I recognize the confusion because the same thing happened in 2007 when I first came to California and some Americans made comments regarding my name. In general, *maki* means roll in Japanese and refers to a sushi roll. With so many Japanese restaurants in California today, Americans have many opportunities to see or hear the word *maki*, and they are familiar with the word. I felt a little strange at first that my name represents a part of Japanese culture to Americans, and I was not so sure about the association with food. One advantage is that Americans can pronounce my name easily, even though the meaning is completely different.

Traditional Japanese female's names often end in *ko*, for example, Akiko, Keiko, Masako, Yoko, and so on. The meaning of *ko* in *kanji* is "a child," but when it comes at the end of a name, it is always a female name. Historically, only the daughters of the imperial family had names ending in *ko*. Then it became popular for many families to honor their own children with imperial names. This custom gave way to another naming tradition beginning around 1980 when parents began to change that style. Now many girls' names do not have *ko*. As a child, I envied those girls with *ko* at the end of their names. I wanted to be like them and blamed my parents for giving me a unique name.

Over the last few decades, popular boys' names also have changed in Japan. Traditionally, parents named their sons with a number in *kanji*. For example, *ichi* means one and was used for names such as Ichiro, which means first son. Another popular name, Jiro, means two or second in *kanji*. In this manner, a man's place in the family was established and confirmed. Families are having fewer children in Japan and attitudes are changing, so it is no longer necessary or popular to have numbers in a boy's name.

My feelings about my name have changed over the years. I believe a name gives a person special identity, and I feel the uniqueness of my name and the identity it gives me. I appreciate my parents for giving me this name.

## Naming Tradition
NANA AFUA SERWAH

*I* AM FROM THE ASHANTI KOTOKO TRIBE in the heart of Ghana, one of fifty-two tribes in the country. Each tribe has a particular way of naming their babies. In my tribe, the Soul Name is the first name given to a baby. The day of week a baby is born determines what soul name the baby will have. Soul names are also different for males and females. For example, if a baby is born on Sunday, the female will be Akosua, and the male will be Akwasi. A male child born on Monday is Kojo, and a female is Adowa. The soul name carries your destiny. I was born on Friday, which is why I'm called Afua, and any male born on Friday is named Kofi. Those born on Friday are thought to be humble and quiet; we don't talk much; we are respectful and have dignity.

We also have a middle name, selected by our parents to honor a special person like a godparent and a last name from our family. The last name is called *den pa*. In my tribe everybody has at least three names, a soul name, a middle name, and a last name. I have five names because I was named after a queen mother of the Ashanti Tribe. We do not call the queens by their names; we give them titles names like Nana, or Maame, which mean mother. Thus, my first name is Nana; my soul name is Afua; my middle name is Kobi, and my last name is Serwah. Then, I have a royal name, Ampem.

The actual naming ceremony takes place eight days after the baby is born. This ceremony is especially significant because it affects the spirit of our soul. Everybody attending the ceremony wears white, black and white, or blue and white, including the baby. The father of the baby will choose the elder from his family to perform the naming ceremony.

Sometimes the father can name the baby either after himself or a friend who has done something great for him. The father is responsible for the baby because in my tribe if the man pays the engagement price of the woman, everything that comes from the woman belongs to the man. It is like they sell the woman to him, but if something unfortunate happens to her, her family will hold him responsible. So, the baby will receive his family name, called the *den pa*, which is also known as the surname of the baby.

The naming ceremony begins at six o'clock in the early morning and ends at six o'clock in the evening. In the morning, both families arrive at the father's house to pour libations and to invoke our ancestors. The elder of the father's family will say the soul name and surname of the baby to the guests at the ceremony for the first time. At the ceremony, there are two cups, one contains water and one contains alcohol. The elder of the family will hold the baby and dip one finger in the water and put it on the baby's tongue. He repeats, "This is water" three times to the baby. Then the same procedure is repeated but with alcohol instead of water. The elder dips the baby's finger in the alcohol and repeats, "This is alcohol." This part of the ceremony demonstrates that the world is full of mysteries and our lives will sometimes be good and sometimes things in our lives will be bad. When life gets bad, we must not give up, but force ourselves to be strong in the world. When the elder completes this ceremony, the remaining water and alcohol will be shared among the family members. This traditional performance was important for my family when I had my three children in the United States.

Gift-giving is an important aspect of the ceremony. The first gift presented is always from the person whom the baby was named after. He or she will put a ring on the baby's finger and money in the baby's hand to symbolize appreciation for the honor of having a child named for him or her and to show respect for the family. Then all of the guests will offer their gifts to the baby. Each gift welcomes the new baby into our tribe.

The celebration is festive and the food delicious. African drummers play, and we have a dance called *Adowa*; everybody dances in a circle with the baby. The celebration includes traditional African food, such as *banku* and okra stew, *fufu* and soup, rice balls and peanut butter soup. Participants eat, drink, and dance until sunset.

## Chinese Family Conflict
JESSICA ZHU

WHEN A NEW BABY IS anticipated, everyone in the family begins to think about the baby's name. Parents and grandparents hope to have a part of their connection to the new baby reflected in the child's name.

The Chinese name generally consists of three parts: the first name, the middle name, and the family name, which is passed down from the father's family. In Chinese tradition, only boys are considered to be true members of the family. Girls will become part of their husband's family after marriage and are thus viewed as temporary or less significant family members. This tradition has been more complicated since 1979 when the Chinese government announced the one-child policy. Right now, all families from the last two generations have one child. This new baby will be the only child and the only grandchild for three families: the parents, the maternal grandparents, and the paternal grandparents. They all want to be involved in selecting a name for the baby. This situation can result in arguments and hurt feelings because each family wants something different from this new child.

For the maternal grandparents, from the mom's side, naming the baby provides a chance to bond with the baby. In Chinese culture, when the grandparents get older, a child or grandchild cares for them. Traditionally, men care for their parents or grandparents since they are officially family members. A married woman has to take care of her husband's parents first. Then she can care for her own parents. Consequently, the maternal grandparents feel the loss a daughter after her marriage and worry about who might care for them in their old age. They hope to choose a name for the grandchild and thus build a relationship with the new child for the future. They are satisfied if one name from their side of the family is used as the baby's middle name or first name to encourage the relationship with the grandchild. For example, if the grandpa's name is Jun Pei Bei, the baby's name could be Jun Huang, with Jun as part of the grandfather's name.

The paternal grandparents have the responsibility of naming the baby as a family member. They usually want to follow traditional Chinese custom to protect the family name for each generation. All the grandchildren in each generation have the same family name passed down from the father's side, and all of the grandchildren have the same middle name, which is selected by the oldest grandfather. The new baby's paternal grandparents choose the first name for the baby. They want a name with a special meaning, such as luck, health, wealth, or a long life. For example, one grandfather named his grandson Bai He, which means long life and perfect poise.

The parents also have a special part to play in naming their baby. The name must be one that they want. This is their first and perhaps only opportunity to name a child because most children in China are only children now, so they attach great importance to their child's name. The parents want a name with a particular meaning that reflects their understanding of the world and their values. Parents might prefer a name that means intelligence or a name related to both parents' families. For example, a girl might be named Cong; *Cong* means smart or clever or ingenious. They might combine this with the name Suo Chen where Suo is the family name passed from the father's side, and Chen has the same pronunciation as the mom's family name but with a different meaning. The parents give their child a part of themselves by selecting a meaningful first name, and honor their parents with the middle and last names.

The one-child policy strongly affects the family culture and the three families who want to name a child for different reasons. The naming of a new baby may end with an argument or an agreement. The name may be taken to show respect for the family that pays all the bills or to show respect and affection for some particular relative. Often someone may feel like a winner and someone else might feel like a loser in the naming process. The naming process has roots in both traditional and modern Chinese culture and reflects the values of each family.

# Chinese Names in Taiwan

EUNMI JYEN

BIRTH REPRESENTS THE BEGINNING OF life, and the birth of a new baby brings great joy to the families and delights the parents. Naming the baby is a difficult mission for parents in Taiwan where superstition in common and deeply grounded in the culture. Superstition plays a significant role because names can affect a baby's future. Naming is also difficult because the Chinese writing system has more than ten thousand characters to choose from.

It is interesting to look at how Chinese people select characters and arrange them into names for their children. My name is Enmien. *En* means gratitude, and *mien* means sheep. I was born into a Christian family, and my name has a Christian meaning, the lamb of grace. This is a very unusual name in Chinese, a name that no one else in the world has.

In my grandparents' generation, parents chose names that had an awkward or unpleasant sound because they believed that if a child had a name that was unpleasant to the ear, the child would grow up to be obedient and have a good personality. For that reason, some unpleasant names were very popular. The name Zhao Di was popular for little girls; it means get a little brother and reflects the cultural preference for boys. These days more fancy, charming, and original names are much more popular because we say our names in public and have them on identification cards.

Many people in Taiwan consult a fortune teller to get help selecting a baby's name. The fortune teller makes predictions about the baby's future and helps parents select a name that suggests the qualities that the parents want the child to have. The predictions are based on the meaning of the Chinese characters as well as on the number of strokes required to write the character. Parents select characters that have meanings like gold, success, champion, or grandeur. For example, one friend's name is Guan Ting, which means champion. Another friend is Mei Hue, which means glorious. These are very popular names, so sometimes children are sitting next to someone who has the same name in class. In a small group of friends, it is not unusual for several people to have the same name.

In Taiwan, naming is like a blessing from the parents. They believe that the names will influence the child's life by helping the child to be obedient, good, and happy. Thus, selecting the perfect name is a challenge for parents. I am grateful for my name. It is unusual and meaningful. My name is distinctive and it fits me very well.


## My Family's Traditions
ARACELY GODINEZ

MY FAMILY HAS A UNIQUE tradition for naming new babies. We have a long tradition of selecting a name from the Bible. This tradition began with my grandparents who named all of their children, my aunts and uncles, with names from the Bible. This was my grandfather's idea and has continued to my generation where all of my cousins have names from the Bible.

When my parents were expecting their first child, my grandfather suggested the name Ishmael for the new baby. This is a beautiful name and has a beautiful meaning, servant of God. My parents were very enthusiastic about the name, and my oldest brother is Ishmael. Three years later, when my second brother was on the way, my parents began to look for a biblical name for the new baby. They decided on Israel because it means nation of God. They also wanted both boys to have names that begin with the same letter.

Biblical names were important to my parents for my brothers, but when they had girls, they changed the tradition. My two sisters and I have beautiful names that begin with the letter A: Aracely, Arely, and Anallely. My parents love both the sound and the look of these names, and so do we.

My parents also have a unique idea about middle names. Most people have multiple names, or at least they have a middle name, but my parents did not give us middle names. I appreciate my parents' combination of family tradition and their own traditions when they gave us our names. When I have children of my own, I anticipate choosing a name from the Bible, perhaps for both boys and girls. I want to keep that part of the family tradition.

CHAPTER FOUR

# Special Birthdays

# Special Birthdays

## First Birthday
ANONYMOUS

*Dol*, THE CELEBRATION OF THE first birthday in Korea, is a very special event. At first glance, it might look like an ordinary birthday party, but it has special meaning and includes several unique parts. In order to commemorate their baby's first birthday, parents busy themselves with elaborate plans for a huge party. In the past, parents held this party in their home and prepared all of the food themselves. In contemporary Korea, the traditional, homey party is often replaced by special-order rice cakes and an expensive dinner in a restaurant rented for the *Dol* celebration. At the party, the baby wears traditional Korean clothing, looking like a little prince or princess, and performs in a very special event called *Dol-Jabi*.

The *Dol* party dates to a time when, because of illness and limited medical knowledge, many infants died before reaching their first birthday. In the olden days, if a baby survived that first year, people assumed the baby would continue to grow healthy and strong. What joy parents and other relatives felt in celebrating *Dol*, a special child's first birthday! The whole village would be invited to the party. Faraway relatives of the baby would travel great distances to attend. The parents would announce the arrival of the baby as a member of the family.

In more modern celebrations of *Dol*, many of the traditional practices are still followed. The baby's parents prepare large amounts of delicious foods such as *gal-bi-jim*, *jab-chae*, and *jeon*. One food that is an absolute necessity at a *Dol* party is red bean cake made with honey and sorghum. The cake is red in color to get rid of bad ghosts. Guests bring presents for the baby, usually clothing or toys. Relatives, though, tend to give a gold ring to symbolize wealth and a healthy life for the baby. To show their gratitude, the parents present the guests with a gift of special rice cakes.

The highlight of the party is *Dol-Jabi*. For this event, parents gather particular objects such as pencils, yarn, and money. The objects are displayed in front of the one year old with the adults predicting the baby's future based on the object she grabs first. Each object has special significance. Pencils indicate a scholarly life with a job such as a professor or lawyer. Yarn symbolizes a long, healthy life. Money means the baby will grow to be a wealthy person. Some young parents today try to use tricks during *Dol-Jabi*. For example, they might add other objects such as a golf ball or a stethoscope or any other object that symbolizes the parents' ardent wishes for their child's future life. A grabbed golf ball might mean a life as a professional golfer, a grabbed stethoscope, a life as a respected physician. Even trickier parents might put the object they want their baby to choose very, very close to the baby. In any case, whatever the baby picks during *Dol-Jabi*, this event gives everyone a good laugh at the party.

Another special part of the modern *Dol* celebration is picture taking. After the party, the parents take their one year old to a photo studio where the child becomes a fashion model, posing for pictures in many different outfits from traditional Korean clothing to a formal suit or dress. Even though the parents are not royalty, their baby becomes a prince or princess for that day in the pictures. It is, however, a tough day for the baby.

I believe that each birthday is an important and meaningful milestone in every person's life. However, in my country, the first birthday is even more special. With many people attending a *Dol* party to wish a family a happy, healthy, and rich future for their child, what a beautiful tradition it is!

## Shichi-Go-San
YUKIKO EGAWA

IF YOU VISIT JAPAN IN the middle of November, you might see many young children at shrines, wearing beautifully crafted kimonos. They are celebrating *Shichi-Go-San*, a traditional Japanese ceremony for children of the ages of seven, five, and three. In fact, the ages of the children celebrating *Shichi-Go-San* correspond with the name of the holiday, which literally translates to seven-five-three in English. Alongside these well-dressed, eager-faced youngsters stand their entire families, who go to a shrine to pray for a healthy life for their children. Originally, *Shichi-Go-San* was celebrated on November Fifteenth, though nowadays many people celebrate it on one of the weekends either before or after the traditional date. Wearing a kimono or formal dress and eating *chitose-ame* are the highlights of this ceremony for Japanese children, and pictures from the celebration will become family keepsakes.

For many children, just the act of wearing a kimono proves to be the most fascinating aspect of this celebration. This traditional Japanese clothing, worn for the first time at the age of three, symbolizes the end of a child's infancy and an initiation into early childhood, a time when he or she is expected to be nice and more mature. At the age of three, we celebrate *Shichi-Go-San* for both boys and girls. After that, we celebrate the age of five for boys and seven for girls. After the age of three, many girls begin to grow their hair long in order to have a nice kimono hairstyle for their seven year old celebration. The age of five is the special occasion for boys to wear a traditional kimono with a *haori* jacket and *hakama* trousers, just like the Japanese Samurai warriors of old. In addition, they proudly carry a toy sword, *katana*.

For seven year old girls, *Shichi-Go-San* is a really special day. They wear very beautiful kimonos, often handcrafted, with makeup on their faces and their hair styled in a special way with *kanzashi*, a hair ornament that matches their kimono. In one hand, they carry a cute handbag made of kimono cloth, and on their feet, they wear *zouri*, a type of Japanese sandals. In the end, these girls look very beautiful, like a bride or princess in an old Japanese castle. They are proud of themselves and walk like real princesses. When I was three years old, I wore my own kimono, made by my grandmother's skillful hands. I was lucky as she was a professional kimono maker. At seven, although my body had almost doubled in size, I could wear that same one I had worn four years earlier because kimonos can be adjusted for growth.

In contemporary Japan, some children prefer to wear formal Western suits or dresses instead of kimonos for *Shichi-Go-San*. Since we don't have Halloween in Japan, this is a good opportunity for boys to don elegant tuxedos and for girls to dress up like princesses from fairy tales. For parents, choosing Western clothing for their child's *Shichi-Go-San* is actually more economical than buying a kimono or having one made for the celebration. Beautiful kimonos are very expensive, even for small children. A brand new kimono for *Shichi-Go-San* costs three hundred dollars or more. Although parents can rent one for the day of the ceremony, they would still need to spend another one hundred dollars for an appointment at the beauty salon, where children have their hair done in a special style to complement the kimono. The salon also ensures that the child is properly dressed in his or her kimono since busy, modern Japanese families tend to wear Western clothes, such as T-shirts and pants, and have not learned the intricacies of putting on a kimono themselves. These aspects of the modern *Shichi-Go-San* celebration show the difficulty of keeping our traditions alive.

In addition to wearing kimonos or other formal clothing to mark the end of infancy, eating *chitose-ame* is another important symbol of *Shichi-Go-San*. *Chitose-ame* means one thousand year old candy in Japanese. Children eat this special candy to have a long and healthy life. The stick-shaped candy is one and a half centimeters in diameter and twenty to thirty centimeters long. This unusually long candy symbolizing long life can only be purchased in

November for *Shichi-Go-San*. There are a few pieces of the special candy in a bag, and each piece is colored either red or white, lucky colors in Japanese culture. The bag the candy comes in is also designed especially for this celebration and is decorated with pictures of cranes and turtles. These illustrations recall a famous Japanese saying: "The crane lives a thousand years, and the turtle lives ten thousand years." These creatures are seen as symbols of long life. I still remember eating that candy after my celebration. It didn't taste very sweet like Western candies, but I liked it because I could eat and enjoy it for a long time.

Other important items related to *Shichi-Go-San* are the photographs of the children who are celebrated. These pictures are special for Japanese people. Since parents want their children's *Shichi-Go-San* pictures to be taken professionally, November is the busiest month for Japanese photographers. At my own three year old celebration, my picture was taken by a professional photographer for the first time. In the picture, I had short hair as I do to this day, but I sported a big, beautiful ribbon on my head. Recently, I showed the picture to my two sons. I thought I looked like a delicate doll in my picture of my long ago self. My kids, however, said I looked like a boy. Although we had been living in the USA for several years, I had my younger son's *Shichi-Go-San* picture taken. When he was five years old, we went back to Tokyo for summer vacation. At that time, my mother's friend loaned us her son's kimono, so he could wear a beautiful boy's kimono with *haori* and *hakama*. Even without a katana, he was very happy to be a little Samurai.

*Shichi-Go-San* is an important day for the Japanese. Parents pray that their children have a long healthy life, and children experience Japanese tradition by wearing kimonos and tasting *chitose-ame*. Even though some children now wear Western clothing for *Shichi-Go-San*, they can still experience the day as it was celebrated in the old days in Japan, clutching their bags of *chitose-ame*, walking alongside other kids wearing the more traditional kimono. Although the celebration just lasts for a day, pictures of the dressed-up children will remain as family treasures for a long time. As my two sons are growing up in the USA, they are more familiar with American culture than they are with Japanese. However, I'd like them to experience Japanese culture as much as possible. I hope someday they will appreciate their Japanese roots, for they have a Japanese mother. Since I live outside of Japan, I realize more and more the importance of stoking the flames of our ancestors' traditions. We have such a beautiful and unique culture, and *Shichi-Go-San* is just a small part of that.

## Quinceñera

LAURA VAZQUEZ

IN MÉXICO, THERE ARE FEW special birthday celebrations, but one that is very famous is called *quinceñera*, referring to girls celebrating their fifteenth birthday. The parents of the *quinceñera* throw a party in honor of their daughter, and the entire extended family and many friends join in the festivities. Some families even plan the *quinceñera* party a year or two in advance in order to get every detail perfect. On the day of the party, the *quinceñera* wears a very beautiful dress similar to a bride's. Most families buy the dress from a store that specializes in wedding gowns, *quinceñera* dresses, and clothes for other special occasions.

It is rare that the *quinceñera's* mom knows how to make a fancy dress like that, but if she does know how, she will sew the dress herself. Traditionally, the *quinceñera* dress was made of white, pink, or cream color fabric, but not anymore. These days the *quinceñera* picks a color she likes, anything from purple to orange to green, for her gown. The parents usually rent a limousine to transport the *quinceñera* from her house to the church and from the church to the place where the party will take place.

Before the party, there is a religious ceremony in honor of the *quinceñera*. Her parents offer a mass for her, thanking God for letting their daughter turn fifteen years old. Her family, friends, and *chambelanes* attend the ceremony with her and her parents. The church overflows with flowers, and its main aisle is decorated with a long red carpet and a special bouquet of flowers tied with a big bow. The bouquet and the bow are usually the same color as the *quinceñera's* dress. After the priest welcomes the guests and gives a blessing, the *quinceñera* walks down the aisle of the church with her family, one parent on each side, her siblings and *chambelanes* following behind. They walk slowly and elegantly to the front of the church, and after they are seated, the priest says a beautiful, moving mass. He talks about life, how wonderful it is to turn fifteen, how the *quinceñera* is starting a new stage in her life.

After the ceremony in the church, there is a big *quinceñera* party. Some families have a lavish buffet for their guests while others offer two or three delicious dishes. When people have finished eating, the announcement comes that the *quinceñera* is going to dance. Usually, there is a DJ for the music, but sometimes it is a live band instead. The first dance is for the *quinceñera* and her father. Before the dance, her dad may put her first pair of high heeled shoes on her feet, and he will dedicate the dance to her. Sometimes her dad will also give her one last doll as they dance to another song called "The Last Doll." These dances represent the idea that the *quinceñera* is not a baby anymore and is now beginning a new chapter in her life.

Once she finishes dancing with her father, the *quinceñera* dances with the *chambelanes*, her formal escorts for the evening. The escorts are usually her brothers, cousins, and friends. There are usually fifteen *chambelanes*, one for each of the *quinceñera's* years. These opening dances are usually ones that have been practiced for months before the party. When the *quinceñera* has finished dancing with the *chambelanes*, the DJ or band announces that the dance floor is open for everybody. People dance and laugh and have a good time. After an hour or so of dancing, the cake is cut and cheers are offered for the *quinceñera*. After the cake, there is more dancing with family and friends until the party is finally over. This day stays in a *quinceñera's* memory for the rest of her life.

Unfortunately, I did not have a *quinceñera* because my parent didn't have money for that, but I went to my cousins' *quinceñeras*, which were fantastic. I helped my cousins choose their dresses, look for a place for their party, and decorate the church. I even practiced all their opening dances with them. I have fond memories of helping my cousins prepare for and celebrate their fifteenth birthdays, but I always wish that I had had my own *quinceñera*.

# Eighteen!

ANNA-LENA NASSAR

ALL OVER THE WORLD PEOPLE celebrate their birthdays, though the nature of the celebration depends on their cultural traditions. In Germany, like in other countries, there are certain birthdays that get celebrated more intensely than others because of their special meaning.

The day of a person's birth is the first special event in life which, of course, the parents of the newborn celebrate. However, the most important birthday for young people in Germany is the day when they turn eighteen years old. This birthday is probably comparable in importance to the twenty-first birthday in the United States. In Germany, the age of eighteen has such a special meaning for teens that they are looking forward to this age the most. It is the day young people turn into adults. It is literally the end of one chapter and the beginning of the next because many changes in daily life are related to this age.

The most important aspect of turning eighteen in Germany is the change in personal rights. At eighteen, people are allowed to enter clubs in the evening, buy and consume all kinds of alcohol, drive a car on their own, and sign legal documents by themselves. Indeed, the most important change at eighteen is becoming responsible and independent in all kinds of decision-making in the eyes of the law.

Besides getting treated differently by law, other people start changing the way they interact with eighteen year olds. It is as if the older adults start taking the young adults more seriously, treating them as grown ups from that day on. But with this new treatment comes the expectation that the new adults will behave differently as well. The teenage years are considered over, and maturity, independence, and prudence should prevail.

As you can see, there are many reasons for celebrating the eighteenth birthday as a special event in life. My own eighteenth birthday was something very special indeed. Ever since I was a child, I have loved Disneyland Paris. I had been there many times because it was only about a seven-hour drive away from where we used to live. My parents and I enjoyed every visit we made there. Two days before my eighteenth birthday, my parents surprised me with my special birthday event. I remember my parents and I were eating dinner in the living room. Seemingly out of nowhere, my mum said I had better finish eating quickly and start packing my things for a three-day trip. I had to think for a moment, and then suddenly, it was clear. I guessed what she meant, but when my father advised me to set my alarm for 2:00 am, I was absolutely sure that we were going to spend my eighteenth birthday in Disneyland Paris. I was so happy that I couldn't wait to get up again and start the trip. My parents hadn't said anything about these plans earlier; consequently, I was very excited and could hardly fall asleep that night.

As arranged, my parents and I got up at 2:00 in the morning, packed our bags and snacks for the car ride, and started driving in darkness. It was in the middle of the night, but we didn't care and couldn't wait to arrive at Disneyland Paris. As with our other trips there, we made it to Paris later that morning before the park opened, a whole day of fun and adventure still in front of us.

The first day was already awesome, full of riding carousels, eating lots of food, and buying Disney souvenirs. After sleeping deeply in one of the nice Disney hotels,

I woke up the next morning to find that my parents had decorated a table and piled presents on top of it. That morning was my actual eighteenth birthday. I got all kinds wonderful gifts and I was grateful for every single item. After having breakfast, we went into the park until lunchtime. Then we went to a nice shopping center close to Disneyland, had a coffee at Starbucks, and enjoyed the rest of the afternoon shopping for nice clothes. In the evening, my parents took me to dinner at a very fine restaurant where we enjoyed the last hours of that day eating lots of delicious food and desserts.

Our last day began, and unfortunately, we had to say goodbye to Disneyland. Sitting in the car packed with Disney bags and listening to a new Disney CD, we started our ride back home. I had an awesome time with my family, and I will always remember this trip as a very special celebration of my eighteenth birthday. When I arrived home, I was excited about the changes in my life that would unfold from that day forward. I was most looking forward to being able to drive on my own because I had already had my driver license for a year, but I could not legally drive without my parents until the age of eighteen. This change gave me a great feeling of independence. In fact, I could drive to school and didn't have to wait for the bus anymore. I had been looking forward to this for a long, long time. Additionally, I could plan my day on my own as needed, driving to parties, meeting up with friends, going to the grocery store or roaming the city without asking my parents to give me a ride or having to take the bus or train. Furthermore, I was able to sign legal forms by myself, and I could buy alcohol wherever I went and whenever I wanted. I could go out with my friends to every club I had ever wanted to visit, making my weekends more fun and exciting.

All in all, I can say that the age of eighteen is something special in Germany because it changes people's rights and gives young people a feeling of independence. I myself experienced turning eighteen as a special event, which I will always keep in mind as a day that changed many parts of my life in a positive way.

## Coming of Age
TAK

WE JAPANESE HAVE MANY SPECIAL celebrations so that people in society can be connected with each other. *Seijin-shiki* or Coming of Age Day, celebrated on Monday of the second week of January, is one such custom. Under Japanese law, twenty is the age that children become adults. Upon reaching twenty, people can vote, enter into contracts, and take on other adult responsibilities. Twenty year olds all over Japan mark this coming of age during *Seijin-shiki*, and millions of people join them, remembering and celebrating their own *Seijin-shiki* every year. In Japan, there are several customs related to the celebration of *Seijin-shiki*.

First of all, people have to prepare what they will wear for the celebration. Though there aren't any rules about specific clothing for *Seijin-shiki*, most young men buy or borrow suits while most young women wear a kimono, a traditional type of Japanese clothing. The suits that the young men wear tend to be traditional black with a white shirt underneath, but the guys will often put on a colorful tie to show their individuality. The young women's kimonos have so many colors and patterns, everything from snowy white cherry blossom to deep pink camellias. The young ladies also place a favorite comb in their hair and carry a *kinchaku*, a traditional Japanese money pouch. The reason that these twenty year olds dress up is to show that they have become adults and are ready to don the clothing of adulthood.

Once dressed appropriately, young people gather at city halls, in huge parks, or in civic centers to hear the mayor's lecture on how they should behave as responsible adults. This speech event is the most important part of *Seijin-shiki*. Some cities even ask big celebrities to make speeches in order not to bore the new adults. There is also entertainment: shows, magic tricks, and comic dialogues. During the ceremony, the new adults take photos with their families and friends, having the pleasure of being reunited on this special day. At the end of the event, twenty year olds receive a memento. In my own case, I got a signet with my name carved on it, signifying that I was old enough to make deals and sign contracts with other people.

In addition to those events, the twenty year olds usually have a party, not one at home, but rather someplace out, like a bar or saloon. After changing out of their suits and kimonos, the new adults put on their everyday clothes to show off the fact that they are eligible to drink and smoke. For some, hanging out and partying with friends is the best part of the day.

In conclusion, Japanese people mark their coming of age by participating in *Seijin-shiki*, a day in which each event marks one of the many steps they will take toward adulthood.

# Birthday Memories

MARYAM FORTANI

THE BIRTHDAY MEMORIES LAID DOWN in this essay are partly family traditions and partly cultural customs. Since I left Iran twenty-seven years ago, I am not sure if these customs are still currently practiced there, but I am sure that my best memories of childhood are my birthday parties.

As far as my memories allow me to go back, my parents had this strange, awful custom of making sure that I had my picture taken at a photography studio around my birthday. My mother would buy a cake and take me and the cake to the photographer. I would sit across the table from the big chocolate cake and pose for the camera, all the while my mind fixed on a visualization of devouring a huge piece of that delectable cake in front of me. My parents and the photographer would try hard to produce a second Mona Lisa smile on my face. They would make me turn my head to the left then to the right, finally deciding just to keep it more or less in the middle. They would implore me not to stare at the camera and encourage me to smile naturally. But by that time, I had visualized eating not just a huge piece but also the entire chocolate cake at least one hundred times. The look on my face was not a sweet smile but a drooling hunger. Despite multiple failures to produce a perfect shot of me and my cake, my parents kept that custom until I was nine years old. At that age, I was sure adults had very strange ways of enjoying birthday celebrations. Now, however, I enjoy looking at those pictures and am grateful for all those efforts that my parents made to make my birthdays so special.

It was the custom in my family to celebrate birthdays on the evening before the actual birthday; however, if that evening fell in the middle of the week, the celebration would be postponed until the first Thursday evening after the birthday. The reason for this is that Fridays are the day off in Iran, so a Thursday evening is comparable to a Friday evening in the USA. As birthdays were generally celebrated at home, we also had to plan in advance how to entertain all the guests.

I invited my school friends and children in our neighborhood to my birthday parties. Typically, there would be fifteen to twenty kids. My mother would prepare the meal herself and order two cakes. My brother, Behzad, my cousins, and I would decorate the house with colored paper and balloons and carefully plan every detail of the entertainment and games to be played. In the early evening, around 5:00, my guests would start to arrive. We would begin with games such as *cheshmbandi* where a blindfolded player used sounds to find other players. The blindfolded player would listen carefully for the others who were trying to be as quiet as possible as they moved around the room. When the blindfolded player caught someone, that person would be blindfolded for the next round.

Another game we used to play at my birthday parties was *sandal bazi* which is very similar to musical chairs. Chairs were set in a circle, the number of chairs one less than the number of players. Upbeat music on a cassette player signaled that players should move around the circle of chairs. When the music, stopped everyone fought for a seat. The player standing was out, one chair was removed from the circle, and the game continued until the most exciting final round with just two players vying for one seat.

When *sandal bazi's* final round was finished, the cake would appear and candles would have been put on and lit. While I blew out the candles, everyone would sing the

Persian version of the happy birthday song. It was also the custom to have one candle less than your actual age on the cake. In other words, if you were turning nine, you would have eight candles on your cake. This was symbolic in a sense because by blowing out the candles, you were blowing out the last eight years of your life and entering your ninth year. The number of candles correlated with the number of years you had aged. Even after you blew out the candles, you would still not be honored as a nine year old. My mom used to tease me by saying Maryam is eight years and three months old or eight years and six months old. Imagine waiting all year long to be one year older, to hopefully have more freedom like staying up late, eating ice cream at night, or riding your bike three streets further away, and still you had to struggle to convince others that you were now nine years old and not eight years, eleven months and thirty days old. The only exception to the above custom was the birthday celebration for twelve month olds when the parents lit one candle.

After the cake was served, I would open the presents and thank all my friends for sharing my special day with me. Soon after, they would head back home. However, like most other Iranians, my family loved food and sought excuses to celebrate into the night. So, after the children had left, the real birthday party would start. The relatives would show up, the house getting full by around 10:00 in the evening. There would usually be about forty adults and fifteen cousins in the house. Food and cake would be served followed by singing, dancing and card playing.

I cannot write about my birthday parties and not write about Abdullah, one of my oldest uncles, and the funniest guy I have ever met in my life: creative, gentle, artistic, and fun to be around. He would always come up with new games.

One of the games we used to play was called swimming, a card game that he said he learned from his German son-in-law. His daughter was married to a German and lived in Germany, and Abdullah had made several trips there. After each trip, he would introduce us to new games and new forms of entertainment. Later in my life I realized the game he called swimming was the game Germans call canasta. I do not remember anymore how the game is played, but I remember we all could play.

While we were playing, Abdullah would sit and draw caricatures of the players with each one involved in some sort of water sport like boat riding, water skiing or swimming. Depending on the stage of the game, if a player was about to lose, his or her caricature would look like he or she was drowning. At the end of the game, everybody had a set of caricatures where all were drowning except for the winner. Abdullah died a year ago at age ninety. I wish I had seen him before his death, and I wish I had kept at least one of those caricatures. Even though Abdullah's death made me very sad, my joyful memories of him on my birthdays still put a smile on my face. When I look back at those special birthday times, I remember happy, loving and affectionate faces. I feel the joy and the closeness I had with all those people around me. Life seemed so simple, and I was so present in the moment.

After the food was served and another cake was cut, I had more presents to open. I said thank you and gave a kiss for each gift. Saying thank you to everybody was easy, but kissing all my relatives, well, that's another story! I believe that I was a bit shy and uncomfortable kissing everybody and really wished I could disappear with all the presents, of course, and start playing with my gifts and my cousins in my own room.

Around midnight, the whole group started playing bingo. The rule was whichever family lost the game had to make breakfast the next morning. Playing bingo was not much fun for the kids, but we loved the sleep over. Even though they all lived nearby, at least some of my relatives would sleep over. The next day we would have breakfast together, with the losing family waking up early to pick up fresh *barbari*, Persian whole wheat bread, just pulled from a hot oven. They would also prepare *haleem*, a dish comparable to oatmeal but with turkey meat added. Honey, cream, and butter were also put on a long sheet, spread on the floor where we sit together and eat our breakfast.

After breakfast, our guests leave and the birthday party would be over. If we were lucky, though, and it had snowed enough to close down school for the next day, we kids made sure to have another sleep over with the games starting all over again.

# Engagement and Marriage

# Engagement and Marriage

## Something Old, Something New
CHIU-YU WANG

"WILL YOU MARRY ME?" These are definitely the sweetest words in the universe. When I heard these lovely words from deep in his heart, my heart beat excitedly and my body turned warm. The tears fell down from my shimmering eyes and became crystal pearls on his shoulder. This moment could be the realization of a beautiful dream for young women who are eager to step into marriage. Marriage, however, has not always been the same type of fresh beginning of life. My engagement and wedding ceremony were quite different from my parents' because the ceremonies have considerably changed with each successive generation.

Thirty years ago, my parents' engagement and wedding ceremonies had to follow Taiwanese cultural traditions. Their marriage was arranged by my paternal grandfather.

The time from their first meeting to their wedding day was just a few months. But how can couples understand and make a commitment to each other in such a short period of time? Honestly, I still wonder whether my father has said "I love you" to my mom at any point in his life. In my parents' generation, the traditional engagement and wedding ceremonies were very simple but deliberate. My father did not propose to my mother, but their families had come to a consensus on the appropriateness of their marriage. On their engagement day, my father and mother gave a little golden ring to each other in front of family members and then had lunch at home. After the ceremony, my parents asked their parents to choose a lucky wedding date for them. This was a way to show their respect to their elders. The wedding date was chosen based on the lunar-calendar yearbook that recorded lucky and unlucky dates for specific occasions such as wedding ceremonies, business openings, and funerals.

Their wedding ceremony was held three months after the engagement. According to my mom's story, she wore a traditional red silk *chipau* for her wedding dress, which was tight enough to show her perfect shape. I have seen my mom's wedding picture, and I can attest to the fact that she indeed had curves in all the right places. Their wedding followed the traditional customs, which seem boring and old-fashioned to me. They did not have a gorgeous reception, exciting games, or even a special memory.

Luckily for me, the traditional Taiwanese engagement and wedding ceremonies are no longer the only choice in my generation. The romantic proposal I accepted was quite different from my parents' experience. I met my husband on the Internet three years ago. At that time, I was preparing for the TOEFL exam, one of the English proficiency tests recognized by most universities in the United States. I posted a message on my English teacher's online forum in order to find a speaking partner to improve my oral skills. After three months of waiting, I finally received an email from a guy who was born in Taiwan but moved to Argentina when he was six. When he wrote to me, he was living alone in northern California. After talking to him a couple of times, I realized that he was the best friend of my English teacher who also grew up in Argentina. Six months later, we decided to meet in the USA, and we have been in love with each other ever since. On a beautiful summer night in 2007, my husband proposed to me with a ring placed in one of those well-known blue boxes from Tiffany's.

Our beautiful engagement banquet took place in a hotel in Kaohsiung, my hometown in Taiwan. Because my parents and some relatives still hold superstition about the wedding dates, they chose a lucky wedding date for us, November 5, 2007. In traditional Taiwanese culture, the wedding date should not be in July on the lunar calendar because this month is the so-called ghost month. My family believed that my marriage would not be happy if the wedding ceremony was held during this evil month.

As the time for our wedding ceremony approached, there were many details to take care of. First, I had to design and write wedding invitations, which consisted of red cards, each printed with a golden Chinese character *xi*, which means happiness in English. Second, my family and I selected wedding cookies and candies, which were placed in round, red boxes with a big *xi* on each lid. These boxes of sweets were given to friends with whom I wanted to share my happiness. Friends of my husband, however, were not allowed to receive these wedding boxes because that was not part of the tradition. In addition, I was not allowed to eat my own wedding cookies because it would bring bad luck to my marriage. Next, my family tasted banquet courses in different hotel restaurants to make sure our guests would have delicious dishes at the wedding reception. Finally, I took sets of wedding pictures with my husband and family in a wedding photo shop. Obviously, these preparations exhausted me, but at the same time, I enjoyed being a blissful bride-to-be.

According to Taiwanese culture, my husband had to go to my house on the morning of our wedding day. He had to thank my parents and promise them that he would take care of me forever. After this traditional farewell ceremony, he took me to the five-star hotel where we had our wedding ceremony. My bridesmaids stayed with me in the hotel room at all times, while my husband had to go to the banquet hall to check every detail and socialize with friends and relatives.

Our wedding ceremony began at seven in the evening. My father and I stood outside the banquet hall and waited for the ceiling lights to go out. Then the bright white light of a spotlight shown down upon us. The bridal march melody played as my father walked me to my groom, who was standing in the center of the stage in the banquet hall, which was beautifully decorated with hundreds of fresh flowers. Once we were on the stage, my groom and I were both very anxious because this was the most important day in our lives. After our parents took turns making brief speeches to us and to the guests, my groom and I exchanged our wedding rings and recited our wedding vows. Then we had the wedding dinner, which consisted of twelve flavorful Chinese dishes; two of the dishes were whole fish and meatballs, both traditional wedding foods in Taiwan. Certain numbers, especially even numbers like twelve and two, are considered lucky, especially for weddings.

When the party was halfway over, I changed out of my snow-white wedding dress into the *chipau* that my mom wore at her wedding. My feelings about wearing this meaningful dress were very complicated because it reminded me that I had already grown up and had more responsibilities ahead in my life. With the *chipau* on, I went with my husband to visit every table and toast all of our friends. At the end of the dinner, our guests were invited to take the leftovers home. This "take-out" behavior might astonish people who are not familiar with Taiwanese customs, but this is a very common custom in Taiwanese society. My husband and I held up a candy tray and stood in front of the exit to wait for our departing guests. As they left, they would say some blessings to us and take some candies home. In our traditional culture, taking wedding candies home is like taking luck with you.

Once most guests were gone, we thought we would have a break; however, this was when the real party began. Our closest friends had previously prepared some exciting and weird games for us. They took out some "tools" such as raw eggs, a scarf, and a blanket. My husband and I knew what was going to happen. We had to comply with our friends' requests; otherwise, we could not get a good night's sleep on our wedding night. One of games made me embarrassed, and I will never forget this mortifying game in all my life. Our friends asked me to roll a raw egg from my husband's right leg to his left leg inside his suit trousers. Maybe you would think this is a piece of cake, but what if a scarf covers your eyes? At the beginning of the game, I carefully used my sense of touch to move the raw egg, and my anxiety increased when the egg reached his "embarrassing area." Everyone was laughing and making loud noises when I touched his "secret spot." I knew what

I had touched but I just tried to stay calm and finished the rest of the game. After this experience, I realized that I had completed the most difficult task at our wedding party and could confront the other challenges as if they were nothing.

When we arrived home after the party, we saw two tangerines that were surrounded by a narrow red strip of paper and six dates on a red fruit tray on our bed; these Chinese cultural symbols prepared by my parents were intended to wish us good luck and fertility in our marriage. Besides this special custom, giving red envelopes is another unique tradition in Taiwan. Taiwanese people give red envelopes filled with money because they think that money is the most practical gift for newlywed couples. My cousin collected our red envelopes as guests arrived at the wedding reception, and she wrote down the guests' names and how much they gave us in a wedding money notebook. If those people get married later, we have to give them a red envelop with more money than they gave us for our wedding. This is an absolutely good investment if you are still single now.

Chinese culture is deeply embedded in Taiwanese society. The majority of Taiwanese people believe that wearing red can keep bad luck away from newlywed couples. Besides the lucky color, avoiding ghost month, using even numbers, and placing a fruit tray on the newlywed's bed are equally important in a Taiwanese wedding ceremony. Taiwanese culture is unique, so many people who are not old-fashioned like me still want to include that culture as part of their wedding ceremony.

# Chinese Wedding Choices

XILEI YAN

WEDDINGS REVEAL THE VALUES AND traditions of Chinese people and are viewed as a gate to another kind of life. There are many different ways of celebrating weddings in China. As you might imagine, the traditional Chinese wedding is somewhat different from a modern Chinese wedding. Today Chinese people can choose to celebrate their special day in the old way or the new way, or they may combine elements of both ways.

On the day of a traditional wedding, both the bride's house and the groom's house are decorated in red. The groom's family sends out a procession of servants and musicians along with a carriage. The carriage is carried to the bride's house on the backs of four servants who will take the bride to the groom's family. When the procession and carriage arrive, the bride will already be dressed in red with a red silk cloth covering her face. In a traditional Chinese wedding, only the groom can see the bride's face. In addition, the groom must carry the bride on his back because the bride's feet cannot touch the ground until she arrives at his house.

When the bride arrives at the groom's house, the wedding begins, witnessed by all their relatives and friends. The bride and the groom worship heaven and earth and the groom's ancestors together, and then bow to each other. After that, the new couple serves tea to all of their elders, and the elders give them red envelopes filled with money. When the ceremony is complete, the groom's family has a feast while the bride waits in the bridal room. After the wedding dinner, the groom enters the bridal room, takes off the red cloth that covers her face, and has a drink with her.

The new couple also eats some candies and peanuts, which symbolize long life and fertility. Some naughty friends of the new couple might also play tricks on them when they are in the bridal room. For example, their friends might ask the bride to cover her eyes and choose her husband by touching the hands of all the men in the room. The bride also asks the groom some questions such as "Will you love me forever?" or "Will you take care of me?" These questions signal the end of the traditional wedding.

The modern Chinese wedding is a little bit different from the traditional one. On the wedding day, early in the morning, the groom and his family decorate a car and drive to the bride's house. At the door, the bridesmaid demands answers to a lot of difficult questions such as "Why should I open the door?" The groom has to answer all the questions in order to show that he is strong enough to take care of the bride. He might even sing out his love for the bride in front of her house before many people gathered around him. Before the bridesmaid will open the door, however, the groom has to promise the money he has prepared for his bride. Finally, he is allowed to enter the house and meet his bride who is dressed in white. The new couple then serves tea to the elders in the bride's family before leaving for the wedding banquet.

The wedding feast is held in a restaurant and is hosted by the parents who want to return their relatives' kindness and to announce the marriage of their children. During the meal, the guests sit at round tables. Sometimes the seating plans are organized in advance so that guests do not have to sit with people they have not met before. After the guests are seated, the bride changes into a red gown, and the new couple goes from table to table, toasting the guests and thanking them for coming. In return, the guests toast the bride and the groom. At the end of the banquet, the new couple stands at the door to thank the guests and wish them well as they leave.

In contemporary society, both traditional and modern Chinese wedding customs are practiced. Because most Chinese people think their wedding is the most important event in their life, they prepare the kind of wedding they want very carefully. I cannot say that one type of Chinese wedding is better than another, but I do believe that Chinese marriage customs are unique, interesting, and reflective of cultural values.

## Getting Married in Cambodia

KUNTHEA MENG

THERE ARE SO MANY COUNTRIES in the world, each with unique languages and traditions. Cambodia, of course, is no exception. Engagement and marriage in Cambodia are wonderful examples of our rich cultural traditions.

The engagement ceremony is celebrated at the woman's house with both families inviting their relatives to attend. The celebration starts in the morning with the man's family bringing *chum noon*—cakes, fruit, and jewelry—to the woman's house. When the families are gathered, they sit around the edge of a red carpet. In the middle of the rug, the man sits opposite the woman. First, the man's parents give the *kan sla* or dowry money to the woman's parents. After that, the man and the woman exchange rings. When the engagement ceremony is over, both families consult a fortune teller to find a sunny, bright, auspicious day for the wedding ceremony.

The wedding ceremony itself is celebrated over two days. The first day consists of the her *chum noon* ceremony. This ceremony begins with a procession from the groom's house to bride's house. Before the procession, the groom's family prepares *pka sla*, a silver tray full of coconut and other flowers, which the groom holds during the procession. The groom's family also prepares silver trays full of fresh fruits, drinks, wine, duck, chicken, pork, and traditional cakes for the wedding. Her *chum noon* begins at seven in the morning, and all the guests are expected to arrive on time for the start of the procession.

When the procession party has assembled, each person holds one tray, with women forming one line of the procession and men forming a second line. The groom, who is carrying the *pka sla*, stands at the front of the two lines. Behind the groom, there are three groomsmen. One of them holds an umbrella for the groom. There are also two little girls and two little boys who hold gold and silver plates. Two teenage girls carry bunches of flowers, and one elderly man serves as a drummer for the procession. When he beats the drum three times, the procession party, with everyone dressed in traditional Khmer clothing, starts its journey to the bride's house.

At the bride's house, they create a wedding hall. In front of the wedding hall, there are two banana trees. The one on the right side is gold, and the one on the left side is silver. On the top of the trees, the bride's family hangs a banner containing the word wedding and the names of the bride and groom. Inside the hall, there are two lines of chairs. Just before the procession party arrives, a red carpet is rolled out between the two lines of chairs. The parents and relatives of the bride stand in front of the wedding hall to welcome the procession.

When the procession party arrives, they enter the wedding hall and sit down in the waiting chairs. Once the guests are seated, the bride comes out to welcome all the guests, especially the groom. The bride and her three bridesmaids wear traditional Khmer clothes as they walk up the red carpet toward the groom. They welcome everyone by exchanging garlands of flowers. When the bride and groom exchange their garland of flowers, they just smile at each other. The final part of her *chum noon* includes gifts for the guests: a shared meal and a bag of bride lace.

When her *chum noon* is finished and most of the guests have left, the first day of the wedding continues with the *sut mum* ceremony, which usually takes place from noon to two o'clock in the afternoon. *Sut mum* is held inside the bride's house with five or six monks who live in the village pagoda. The groom, bride, groomsmen and bridesmaids sit opposite the monks. Behind them are parents and relatives from both sides of the family. When the monks start to pray, the relatives throw fragrant white coconut flowers in the air, filling the house with a beautiful, sweet smell.

After the *sut mum* ceremony, the haircut ceremony is performed. For this ceremony, the groom, bride, groomsmen and bridesmaids sit around a finely decorated table. On the table, there are gold scissors and a gold comb spread out on a gold tray as well as perfumes and bunches of colorful of flowers. The groom's parents pretend to cut the couple's hair because this is supposed to bring good luck to the newlyweds. The haircut ceremony is followed by traditional Khmer music played with drums and flutes.

On the second day of the wedding, all the guests come back to share a meal together. The festivities start at eleven in the morning. To welcome the guests as they arrive, the groom and groomsmen stand on the right side of the wedding hall and the bride and bridesmaids on the left side. At the end of the wedding feast, the couple cuts their wedding cake, and not long after that, they take leave to begin their honeymoon.

In short, getting engaged and married in Cambodia are beautiful examples of meaningful cultural practices.

## Mixing Marriage Traditions

AMORNRAT GAULT

EVERY WOMAN WANTS A DREAM engagement and wedding, and I was no different. I have been engaged and married two times, but to the same groom. I'm Buddhist and my husband is Christian, so we had two weddings. I still remember very clearly the day of my Christian wedding, New Year's Eve 2001 at Hale Koa Hotel in Waikiki Beach. Another happy day of my life was the Thai wedding with my family. My husband and I went back to Thailand and got married again on April 18, 2002, sharing a wonderful Thai ceremony. We decided to start our new life together with the New Year in both cultures, which is why we chose April for our wedding in Thailand where the New Year begins in April.

The Thai wedding is unique, and it used to be more complex with lots of steps to follow. Presently, it has been modified to be more modern and simple. For example, on my Thai wedding day, we had a simple ceremony. My mother's friends came to the house very early in morning to cook and prepare for the wedding. My husband wore a white shirt and blue pants, and I donned an elegant, pink Thai dress. Later in the morning, the monks came to bless us, and after that, we all ate a special breakfast of *met khanoon*, a sweet dish made in a brass wok from peeled split mung beans, eggs, coconut cream, and sugar. *Met khanoon* means jackfruit seed, which is what the dish resembles. At a wedding, *met khanoon* symbolizes the ongoing support for whatever the bride and groom do in life and the wish that they never lose sight of their dreams. Another food we had at our wedding breakfast was *khanom chan*, a dish made from rice flour, tapioca flour, coconut milk, sugar, water, and various natural ingredients such as carrots and taro root which add vibrant color to the dish. For a wedding, *Khanom chan* is shaped into roses to symbolize the bride and groom moving forward in life and building their family.

In the afternoon of our wedding day, we celebrated the traditional *rod-nam-sang* or water blessing at my parents' house. This is the main event of a Thai wedding where both the bride's and groom's family come together to witness this important beginning for a new couple. We call this event *rod-nam-sang* because we soak (*rod*) our hands in water (*nam*), contained in a conch shell container, *sang*. During the ceremony, my husband and I sat close together on the floor with our hands held in a *wai* style to pay respect to the lord Buddha. Chains of crown flowers, jasmine, and roses connected our necks and hands. My parents soaked our hands in blessing water and wished us good luck. Then my relatives, my husband's relatives, and our friends did the same. Everybody wished us good luck for happy lives together, and our ears were full of their wonderful words.

That same evening we had a wedding party in my parents' front yard. There were so many people in attendance that I was not sure I could remember them all. Before the party, I helped my mom and my aunts cook lots of food. My aunts made cocktails once the evening party had begun.

My sister was the mistress of ceremonies, and she welcomed everyone, sang a song, and then opened the floor for all of us to dance. Later my parents honored my husband and me by giving speeches. Both of them wished us a happy life together and gave us some tips for a successful marriage. For example, they told us that marriage is like chop sticks; you need both parties cooperating in order to get things done. They also described spouses as tongue and teeth, each needing the other despite the fact that the teeth may bite the tongue sometimes. A little pain is to be expected in marriage. Their last piece of advice was to be calm and cool in marriage because both characteristics will serve a couple well. After my parents' speeches, we ate, drank, and danced until midnight.

My two weddings were very special to me and our families. I saw the happy smiles on my parents' faces at both ceremonies. I still remember what my parents told me about sharing my life with my husband. Sometimes as I look through the photos in our wedding albums, I see those days in vivid detail, beautiful memories that will never fade from my mind.

## Celebrating Love
STEPHANY ANGRICKA RIRIEN

ENGAGEMENT AND MARRIAGE ARE BOTH special events for every person around the world because those are really big steps in life. Even though you will enjoy other special occasions, few will compare with the beauty and love with which you will be showered on your engagement and wedding days. Every country around the world has its own unique practices and traditions to celebrate those special days, and my native country, Indonesia, is no exception. However, wherever you come from in this world, engagements and weddings are all about one thing: love.

In Indonesia, the first official recognition of a couple's new status happens with the engagement party. This party is usually held a year before the wedding day and is hosted by the parents of the bride. The guest list should include members of both the bride's and groom's family as well as friends. The engagement party is typically a brunch, lunch or dinner held at a restaurant or at the bride's parents' house. The party is usually paid for by the bride's family. In addition to an engagement ring as is common in America, the Indonesian groom will give a necklace to the bride as a symbol of the engagement itself. The necklace can be white or yellow gold and possibly contain gems such as diamonds, rubies, or sapphires. Most women, in fact, prefer to be consulted about their engagement necklace, and some even want to participate actively in its selection. Sometimes the price of the necklace is also a joint decision.

The engagement party is also a good way to introduce the families of the bride and groom to each other so that the relationships between them can be closer. On this occasion, both families will discuss all the planning for the wedding, with a special focus on finding a good day for the marriage itself. Indonesians prefer to have weddings at the end of the year between October and December. This period of time is the rainy season in Indonesia, but it is preferred for weddings because the rain keeps the temperature cool.

After the Engagement party, the bride and groom begin the necessary preparation for their marriage in earnest. There is much to prepare: finding a wedding venue for the reception, finding a place for the religious ceremony, making the guest list, choosing the wedding band, and selecting the caterer, wedding cake and music. Weddings cost a lot of money, and traditionally, the groom's family has been expected to pay for almost everything. However, in contemporary Indonesian society, the sharing of wedding expenses has become more common just as it has in modern America.

About a week before the wedding, an Indonesian couple has another unique tradition which is called *sajit*. The groom's family visits the bride's family with eight trays full of gifts. The number eight is widely believed to be a lucky number. The gifts themselves should contain a full set of new clothing for the bride, which traditionally symbolizes the beginning of the bride's new life as a wife. In addition to this clothing, certain fruits, such as oranges and pears, are given to represent wealth and prosperity. Candies are given as symbols of luck and the sweetness of life, and sticky rice is given with the hope that the families will form a strong bond. The groom also gives a dowry to the bride's parents to show gratitude and offset the parents' expenses for raising their daughter to adulthood. All the trays bearing these gifts must be wrapped in gold and red paper.

The wedding day itself usually starts with a religious wedding ceremony and is followed by a wedding reception. Indonesian wedding receptions are usually attended by an enormous number of guests, between five hundred and two thousand people. This large group of guests is composed of family, friends, neighbors, and colleagues of the bride and groom. It is common for the couple's parents to invite their family, friends, neighbors, and colleagues as well. The reception is usually held in a wedding hall, restaurant, museum or hotel ballroom.

The meal at the reception can be either lunch or dinner, sit-down or buffet style.

Of course, the most important aspect of marriage in Indonesia is not the engagement period or the fancy wedding reception, but rather the time to treasure one another and begin settling into a new life together.

## Arranged Marriage in India
KANDASAMY

THE WAY WE LIVE BEFORE and after marriage is very different, so people around the world call it a life-changing event. However, marriage is celebrated in different ways in different cultures according to their traditions. Marriage is an important traditional event in Indian culture, too. Most Indian marriages are arranged by a couple's parents. Major events in Indian marriages include selecting a bride or bridegroom, matching the couple's stars, meeting the future spouse, celebrating the engagement, finally and wedding ceremony.

The first step in an Indian marriage is for the parents to identify a potential bride or groom for their child. When parents decide it is time for their child to marry, they ask their relatives and close friends to look for a suitable alliance. The bridegroom's parents normally initiate this process; however, the bride's parents also do similar things in certain instances. Once the search for a spouse has begun, relatives and friends come back with a list of potential matches along with photos and horoscopes for each possible match. Parents go through the list and select a suitable woman in consultation with their son. Family status, job, age, education, and appearance are a few things that play a major role in short listing a potential spouse. To give an example close to home, one of my father's friends brought him a marriage proposal for my sister. Our family pursued it successfully, and my sister is now married to a good man.

After selecting a potential bride or groom, the parents' next step is to meet with their astrologer. Astrology, which is part of religious traditions, plays an important role in the decision-making process. The astrologer verifies both the bride's and bridegroom's horoscope and tries to match their stars. If the horoscopes match, then the parents proceed to the next step. Otherwise, the proposal will be dropped at this stage. If the next step is taken, all the communication between both families takes place through a common family member or friend. Having a suitable proposal with matching horoscopes is a major milestone in Indian marriages, but there are still a number of things that must be taken care of before an engagement happens. As a next step, both families meet together at the bride's home. During this time, the potential bride and bridegroom will have an opportunity to meet each other and share their interests. If both find that their interests match and that they have common goals, they inform their parent to proceed in selecting a date for the engagement.

The engagement celebration normally takes place at the bride-to-be's home in the presence of close relatives and friends. According to religious traditions, the bridegroom-to-be's sister formally presents a wedding ring and a chain to the bride-to-be. In the same fashion, the bride-to-be's brother presents a wedding ring to the bridegroom-to-be. On this occasion, the parents announce the wedding date in consultation with the astrologer. This period after the engagement celebration is similar to dating in the western world. The printing and sending of wedding cards to the couple's relatives and friends also follows the engagement. After this, the couple may have the opportunity to talk often.

Indian marriages are usually celebrated for two weeks. During the first week, the couple begins buying clothing and gold and silver jewelry, both major expenses of Indian marriages. Most close family members go along with the bride and groom for this shopping. For example, we had around fifty people who came along with us to shop at the time of my sister's wedding. During the first week, close relatives also gather in the bride's or groom's house to help with preparations such as decorating the house, planning the meal for the guests, and preparing the wedding hall. Wedding halls, where marriages normally take place, are built with kitchens to prepare meals for the guests. In India, it is not surprising to invite one thousand wedding guests, so providing meals for all those people is a great challenge that requires careful planning. While the first week is spent mostly in preparation for marriage, the second week starts with the wedding. Normally, the wedding takes place early in the morning because this symbolizes the dawn of a new life. After the marriage ceremony, the couple visits many temples as per their tradition. Afterwards, the newlywed couple visits close relatives and stays for a few days with each family. This helps everyone get acquainted with the new members in the family.

Indian marriages require a lot of effort and time, but it's really fun to participate and enjoy the many celebrations with family and friends.

# The Steps to Marriage

QAIS H ZARGI

*A* MARRIAGE, THE SOCIAL AND LEGAL relationship between two individuals, takes place in different ways depending on the culture and varies from one culture to another, but most often, marriage is formalized by a wedding celebration. Every culture has a unique process for preparing for the wedding. In Afghanistan, the wedding process begins with a proposal and requires several events for the couple leading up to the wedding day.

When a man decides he is ready for marriage, he has a conversation with his family. This conversation begins the process. The man's parents research the woman's family. They want to know everything about her family's background to ensure that she is the right person for their son. Then they talk to her family so that the families can learn about each other. Once they are confident, they offer the proposal of marriage to her parents. If the woman's family rejects the proposal, his family may try two or three more times. During this period, the woman's family is learning about the man's family background and checking the details for accuracy. When the woman's family accepts the proposal, they give sweets to the man's parents.

When the proposal has been accepted, the man's family offers the sweets from the woman's parents to their guests at a small party. This party is called *Labs Gray*, or proposal acceptance. This party includes only the man's close family and friends. This party makes the proposal official, and the couple can then see each other and go out during the day.

Engagement is the next step. In Afghan culture the engagement is an important part of the wedding. The parents of both the man and the woman get together and schedule a specific date for the engagement party, which includes invited guests with relatives and friends from both families. The engaged couple exchanges rings at this event and all of the guests bring them gifts. The party includes food, music, and dancing. After the engagement party, the couple is allowed to spend time together, but the woman cannot go to the man's home alone. They can never spend the night at each other's homes.

The wedding ceremony is the final step. Both families invite their relatives and friends to the event, which also includes food, music, and dancing, like the engagement party. At the wedding party, they also invite a religious person, a *mula*. During the first half of the party, the woman wears a green gown and must not wear anything black. The man generally wears a brown suit since he also cannot wear anything black. When the couple enters the hall, everyone stands to show respect. After the grand entrance, an older woman from each family performs the henna ceremony. They put a henna design on the right hand of the man and the woman. Friends of the man and woman wear traditional Afghan clothes and dance to traditional music, called *Attan*. After the henna ceremony, both the man and the woman change into their wedding clothes. She wears a white gown and he wears a black suit and black shoes. They enter the hall, sit with both families, and invite the *mula* to recite from the holy *quran* and write the wedding agreement. This is when the couple is united in wedlock. After this, the bride and groom go to the center of the hall and cut the cake. Then they dance together and soon their close relatives join the dance. The party ends with a good night song before everyone goes home.

The final step is called *Taghjami*. This takes place one week after the wedding when the bride's family brings her clothes to her new home and the groom's family prepares food for her family. After this, the bride and groom go on their honeymoon and start their new life.

The Afghan engagement and wedding customs are unique and very interesting. I hope everyone can attend such an event to discover Afghan culture and enjoy the party.

## Modern or Arranged

KONI TAMIRU

*M*ARRIAGE IS A SOCIAL UNION between individuals that creates a relationship. It is a legal relationship between husband and wife, and it is one of the milestones to celebrate in people's lives. In my country, Ethiopia, there are two kinds of marriages: arranged and modern.

Arranged marriages tend to be held in villages, and the couple's parents are responsible for arranging the marriage for their children. With arranged marriages, couples meet for the first time on their wedding day. For instance, my dad was invited by one of his coworkers to go to a friend's arranged marriage. After he came back from the wedding, he told us what happened at the wedding ceremony. He said that the bride's face was covered throughout the ceremony. My dad asked his friend how long the bride had to cover her face. His co-worker told him that she would remain covered until dark. We were all surprised to hear about this practice, but we couldn't do anything about it. We know arranged marriage has bad influence on young children. Even though many Ethiopians are against the idea of arranged marriage, some people still do agree with this practice. However, nowadays more and more men and women, especially those who live in village areas, argue against rural communities following this tradition while still acknowledging that it is important to marry someone the family has accepted and approved of.

In both modern and arranged marriages, the groom, accompanied by his family and friends, goes to his bride's home to take her to the church on their wedding day. When the groom's party arrives, the bride's family and friends hold the door closed and won't let the groom inside to take his bride. In the end, he gets his bride, and his family and friends dance and sing songs before heading to the church. Once in the church, the groom and bride sit on special chairs facing the guests. Each wears a crown and a velvet robe with a big cross on it that was given to them by the church priest. As the priest announces their wish to be married before God, the bride and groom promise themselves to each other, and the church choir begins to sing traditional songs. The choir walks through the crowd, and the bride and groom join the choir and sing along with their family and friends. When the church ceremony is over, everyone walks to the reception while the bride and groom take pictures next to their decorated horses, and their *mize*, the bridesmaids and groomsmen, continue singing and dancing around them.

Some family members and friends go to the reception to welcome guests while the others follow the bride and groom. Some guests carry presents for the bride and groom. Most people carry long, lighted candles. When the bride and groom arrive at the reception hall, the bridesmaids and the groomsmen make an arch of candles for the bride and groom to walk underneath. This arch of candles symbolizes their wishes for the couple to have a bright future. The priest asks the bride and groom to stand and receive his blessing.

The priest prays for the crowd and blesses the food. Next, the couple walks to a decorated table to get food. They are served by their bridesmaids and groomsmen who help to put food on their plates. The food is made with an array of fragrant spices, making the dishes special for the wedding. For example, there is a special sauce called *doro watt* that is made with chicken, onions, garlic, and spices. Other very special dishes are made of vegetables and beef sauces, and of course, there is *injra*, delicious Ethiopian bread. After the food is served, the priest asks the crowned to rise, and the young deacons take out brass rattles and line up facing each other as they sing hymns for the couple. When the singing is done, the groom takes his bride to his family's home.

Arranged marriages in Ethiopia have both positive and negative aspects. The good side is the special ceremony; the bad side is the bride and groom not knowing each other before they get married. But the biggest concern with arranged marriage should be the wellbeing of child brides and grooms. If the marriage of young children is not stopped, there will continue to be serious harm done to these children. I agree with my dad that there needs to be changes in the way parents arrange marriages for their children.

## The Polish Wedding Ceremony
MAGDA PTAK

FROM THE TIME WE ARE BORN, we have so many different occasions to celebrate life and to get together with those we love. Some of these occasions, like being born or dying, are a big surprise, and they can be only once in a lifetime experiences. Other occasions are celebrated every year. Those celebrations are, of course, different in each culture, but they might also vary within the same country or even within the same family. Among the occasions that human beings celebrate, the wedding ceremony is one of the most important, not only in Poland, but all over the world.

I remember when I was fourteen, and my oldest brother got married. Since he was one of the oldest among all the cousins in the family, his was the first wedding of his generation in the family, and everybody was so excited to attend. For me, it was the best wedding I've ever been to. There were about two hundred and thirty people, most of whom were our family and friends that I've known since I was a child. The wedding was in a nice church, and the reception lasted until early Sunday morning and started up again on Sunday afternoon. It was a traditional Polish wedding with all special wedding customs.

Most weddings in Poland are very big and last for a long time. They usually start on Saturday afternoon and last until Sunday morning. Usually this is not enough, however. After a few hours of sleep, guests gather together again on Sunday afternoon to celebrate, but only until midnight this time because next day is Monday, a work or school day for everyone. However, even this is usually not the end of the party because very often the closest family and friends help clean up after the wedding and gather together again on Monday evening to drink and eat the large amounts of food left over from the weekend festivities.

Poland is a largely Catholic country, so usually the weddings take place at the bride's church. A wedding ceremony must be preceded by *zapowiedzi*, a special announcement at church for a few weeks before so that everybody knows who is going to get married to whom. On the wedding day, before the young couple goes to the church, the groom arrives with his parents at the bride's house. He comes all dressed up, holding a bouquet of flowers. Usually there are musicians playing, and when new people approach the home, they play marches and get small tips for these performances.

Before the church ceremony, the close family also gathers at the bride's home to accompany the new couple to the church and see the blessing from their parents. The parents' blessing before the church ceremony is so important that if a mother or father has died, the wedding party stops at the cemetery where the groom or bride can ask for a blessing from the deceased parent. Traditionally, the mother of the bride starts the blessing. She sprinkles the bride and groom with holy water, makes the sign of cross, and gives them a crucifix to kiss. Then the other parents follow her lead. After the blessing, the bride and groom thank, hug, and kiss their parents, and the wedding party prepares to leave for church.

In times past, during the church ceremony, the bride was expected to cry. If she didn't, it was believed that she would cry throughout her married life. Nowadays nobody believes in that, and the bride is always happy and smiling. She might still cry, but only from happiness. There is also a symbolic belief about the order in which a new couple leaves the altar after the ceremony. It can reveal, it is said, who will be more important at home and who will make the decisions.

After the wedding ceremony, there is time for congratulations. As the bride and groom leave the church, the organist plays Mendelssohn's "Wedding March" or "Ave Maria." Everybody waits in a line in front of the church to congratulate the young couple. Then guests usually throw small coins to the young couple, which they need to pick up. This is an old custom, but still very popular. In fact, when I was at the university, my friends and I collected small change in an empty bottle so that we could use it for whoever among us got married first. Sometimes people throw grain or rice at a young couple instead of coins.

Especially in villages and small towns, it is also popular for friends, coworkers, neighbors, and kids who won't be attending the wedding to set up gates for the new couple between the wedding house and the church. The gate can be just a colorful ribbon, decorated with flowers, which is unrolled across a street or something that has a special connection with the couple. People who stand at these gates have flowers for the bride and offer good wishes. Sometimes they dress up so that nobody can recognize them. The best man has to pay the gatekeepers' tolls: sweets if they are children, wedding vodka if they are adults. If there are many gates between the wedding house and the church, it means that everybody likes the new couple and wishes them the best.

When the newlyweds and invited guests arrive at the wedding house, the groom always carries the bride in his arms so that they can step over the threshold together with the hope that this will give them happiness in their marriage. One of the very old customs is that the young couple is greeted at the entrance of the house by the bride's and groom's parents with bread and salt. The parents usually say, "According to our old Polish tradition, we greet you with bread and salt so that your home might always enjoy abundance." With the bread, the parents are hoping that their children will never be hungry, and with the salt, they are reminding the couple that their lives may be difficult at times, but they must learn how to cope with life's struggles. They also give them wine which symbolizes the desire that the couple will never go thirsty and that their lives will be filled with health and happiness. After the bride and groom taste a piece of bread sprinkled with salt, they break a plate and a glass for good luck. The parents kiss them, and then it's on to the start of the reception.

The wedding feast also follows some old traditions. The couple usually sits at the table which is located along a wall containing holy pictures. Always the first dance is reserved for the newlyweds, and after this, everybody is invited to dance. There is always a lot of Polish food and alcohol, and the wedding reception lasts into the early morning hours. Usually, the first course of the wedding banquet is chicken broth with pasta, and then there are potatoes, all kinds of salads and meat—pork chops, fried chicken, chicken chops, meatloaf, and meatballs. There are also desserts: fruit, cakes, gelatins, and candies. As soon as people finish dinner, the waitresses start cleaning the plates and bring more food to the table. This time there are mostly cold cuts, mayonnaise-based salads, and cold fish. In fact, through the whole wedding, the waitresses are bringing new food, and usually people are so full that they can't eat anymore. Very often there are another two soups, red borsch with dumplings and white borsch with sausage and eggs, not to mention the chicken with French fries and mushrooms, the hunter's stew and much, much more. Polish people usually drink shots of vodka or wine. Other drinks are not very popular at weddings.

The most important wedding custom takes place around twelve midnight. It is called *oczepiny* because in the past it was the moment when the *czepek*, the cap of a married woman, was put on the bride's head. This tradition survives to this day, but nowadays it is a little bit different. There is no *czepek* anymore, and the witnesses just take off the bride's veil and groom's bow tie. There are always some special songs and games, like choosing the next couple by throwing the veil and bow tie at single young women and men, or the money dance, where guests have to donate money for the privilege of dancing with the bride or groom. The money is put into an apron, basket, plate, or decorated box before dancing with the bride or groom. After each guest dances with the bride, they may receive a drink and a piece of the freshly cut wedding cake.

Polish weddings certainly differ one from another. Some are just small receptions for close family, and some are for more than two hundred people. Different families and different regions in Poland also have their own special customs, but what is common to each wedding is the parents' blessing before the church ceremony, the salt and bread blessing, and *oczepiny*. Whether large or small, traditional or unique, a wedding is an unforgettable event for the new couple.

## Lost Traditions

YURISLADY RODRIGUEZ

IN EVERY COUNTRY OF OUR world we can discover an enormous diversity of special celebrations, ceremonies, and important events that distinguish one culture from another. Throughout civilizations, people have been honoring births, naming traditions, special birthdays, wedding anniversaries, and engagements and weddings in unique and interesting ways.

In Cuba, the beautiful island where I come from, the culture has changed radically over the past fifty years because of a social, cultural, and economic revolution. Since that time, weddings have stopped being important for many Cubans. For that reason, marriage is not as common as it is in countries with stable social and economic conditions. For many reason there has been a discrepancy between those wanting to marry and those who actually do get married. There are probably many reasons why Cubans don't get married any more, but the most glaring reason is economic. Of course, some Cuban people in the country get married because of their religious beliefs, especially those from a Roman Catholic tradition. Others get married because of their good financial condition and a comfortable way of living, which allows them to afford a wedding. Unfortunately, the majority of Cuban people do not get married at all because their difficult economic situation makes marriage out of their reach.

Today in Cuba, many people are obligated to live together without marriage, to have children together, without marriage. In spite of this, people still live as families in the same house, sharing happiness and sadness as a couple and maintaining the customs of naming their children after their fathers and grandfathers.

Many people wonder why we have lost that beautiful tradition that is considered important in so many other cultures. I have heard many stories from my grandparents, especially my grandmother about how Cuba was before the revolution, before Castro. I have asked many times why my own parents were never married like she was. My grandmother said that when she got married more than sixty years ago, times were very different in Cuba. Everyone had a stable financial situation. They could afford to have the elaborate and festive wedding celebration. Sadly this was not the situation for my parents.

All through my childhood, I wanted to attend a wedding, but I was never so lucky because no one in my family ever got married, nor did anyone in the families of my friends. Consequently, I was always curious about what a wedding was like and how people got ready for a wedding. I wondered what the ceremony consisted of and what the party afterwards was like.

In the early 1990s, the Cuban government paid for weddings, so some people pretended to be in love so that they could have parties with beer, cake, and soft drinks. The government wanted to promote marriage and to gain support for the government. This hypocritical action by the government convinced some people, but this effort did not change the culture significantly. Many people, perhaps most people, still do not get married.

I think it is a shame that Cubans have lost the tradition of marriage through the course of the Castro revolution. We have lost many aspects of our culture, but I am hopeful that one day people will have the desire and the good fortune to get married, a privilege enjoyed in most other cultures of the world.

CHAPTER SIX

# Wedding Anniversaries

25-50-75 in the Philippines

Anniversary Traditions

Celebrating in Brazil

My Grandparents' Anniversary

An Unforgettable Day

Poems and Hikes

# Wedding Anniversaries

## 25-50-75 in the Philippines

RON DIZON

*E*VERY MARRIED COUPLE IN THE world has a way of celebrating a wedding anniversary, which is one of the most important days to remember in a married couple's life. Every year wedding anniversaries are remembered and celebrated by couples, regardless of their financial status. Love and romance are the themes on this special day. In the Philippines, couples often celebrate their first wedding anniversary with their firstborn child whose charm and innocence bring more joy and color to the event. Each year after that first year, a wedding anniversary is not only remembered but also celebrated in some way. The most special wedding anniversary celebrations in the Philippines are the twenty-fifth or silver anniversary, the fiftieth or golden anniversary, and the seventy-fifth or the diamond wedding anniversary.

The silver wedding anniversary, marking the twenty-fifth year of a couple's marriage, is usually celebrated at the house of the couple with their invited guests—relatives and friends. Before the celebration, the couple attends a mass at their church, giving praise and thanks to the Lord for their unwavering love and long marriage. At the celebration, the food is abundant. Rich couples serve luxurious dishes such as *lechon*, a whole roasted pig or calf, shrimp, and mud crabs. Other couples offer simpler dishes such as *adobo*, chicken or pork cooked in soy sauce and vinegar, and local fish like tilapia. Whether rich or poor, every couple includes *pancit guisado*, stir-fried noodles, symbolizing longevity and luck. The celebration usually lasts until midnight and sometimes is even extended to the following day for latecomers. I have attended many of these occasions, and the most unforgettable was my aunt's anniversary on March 20, 1992 when she and her husband kissed for more than a minute at their guests' request. The atmosphere was filled with love and joy.

After the silver anniversary, the next special celebration is the golden wedding anniversary to celebrate fifty years of marriage. This event is not only associated with delicious food and a huge party, but also with another wedding ceremony. Married couples, who are usually in their seventies by this point, renew their first wedding vows "to love each other and live together for richer or for poorer until death do us part." This renewal is done in the eyes of the Lord in a public celebration. A couple's children, who already have their own families and children, are usually the bridesmaids and groomsmen in the wedding. This is a rare event, but in 1998 I attended one. It was my friend Juan's grandparents' anniversary. The ceremony was very touching, inspiring, and a little bit funny because the officiating priest had to speak loudly and repeat some words for the husband.

For a few lucky couples, the golden anniversary is followed by the seventy-fifth or diamond wedding anniversary. Couples who are blessed with good health and a long married life celebrate their diamond anniversary in the same way as the silver anniversary, but this time, there is more of a crowd because the grandchildren have doubled in number, with many of them having already started their own families. The diamond anniversary also has more food and fun because of the added excitement of meeting relatives coming from faraway places. It's like a whole clan reunion. Sometimes, if the family finances permit, a musical band is hired to play music and bring more joy to the event. I saw one of these very uncommon events about 20 years ago, but it was on television. Happiness and joy were still evident on the couple's faces even though they seemed to be not that vigorous anymore. The reception was held in an open basketball court to accommodate the many friends and relatives who had gathered to celebrate the long, successful marriage.

These special wedding anniversaries are celebrated and remembered by married couples for their entire lives. Their sacred vows, "to love each other and to live together for richer or for poorer until death do us part," will remain in them until their last breath and serve as an example of a true and long-lasting love to their descendants.

# Anniversary Traditions

LIUDMILA SKRYPKO

WEDDING ANNIVERSARIES ARE SIGNIFICANT FAMILY events for both parents and children. Celebrating every year together is a symbol of confidence and happiness in the family. In Russia, wedding anniversaries are celebrated every year, and they each have special names, celebration traditions, unforgettable moments, and unusual gifts.

Since the nineteenth century, we have had a special calendar for wedding anniversaries in Russia. In this calendar, it is interesting to note the way each subsequent anniversary symbolizes an evolution of the relationship between spouses, becoming stronger each year. For example, the first year is the chintz anniversary, the second is paper, the third is leather, the fourth is linen, and the fifth is wood. The first five years of marriage are the most difficult for a young family, so we can see how the name for each of the first five anniversaries changes from fragile material like chintz to solid material like wood. For years six through twelve, wedding anniversaries have other names related to metals such as copper, iron, and steel. In this period, the relationship between wife and husband is solidifying, just like metals. Thirteen years together marks the end of forming the foundation of family ties and the beginning of refining the relationship. The anniversaries during the next few years have to be soft like cashmere (thirteen years), reliable like agate (fourteen years), and clear like crystal (fifteen years). After the crystal anniversary, we celebrate every fifth year. The twentieth year is the porcelain anniversary, and the twenty-fifth is the silver. The next five wedding anniversaries have names of the most expensive stones and metals such as pearl, coral, ruby, sapphire, and gold.

In Russia, we also have many interesting traditions to celebrate wedding anniversaries. I remember one very amazing party. When I was ten years old, my parents and I attended my grandparents' golden wedding anniversary. My grandparents brought together all of their six children, fifteen grandchildren and four great-grandchildren. At that time, they had been living together for fifty years, and they were seventy-five years old. My aunts and uncles organized an unforgettable golden wedding anniversary party in a restaurant with beautiful traditions and special ceremonies.

The room for the party was decorated with family pictures, beautiful flowers, and colored balloons. The anniversary table was covered with a white tablecloth, and there were many Russian foods and drinks. When the ceremony began, the "newlyweds" were sitting at the center of the table, and all the guests sat to the left and right of them. Everyone was wearing very beautiful clothes. My grandfather dressed himself in an elegant black suit; my grandmother wore a long white dress, her grey hair neatly styled in a classic bun. According to tradition, the first ceremony of the golden anniversary was exchanging new golden rings which the children bought for their parents. It was a magnificent moment! Two old people in wedding clothes put new rings on each other's hand, and then the "groom" kissed the "bride" just as he had done fifty years ago. In this moment, I saw love and tenderness in my grandparents' eyes. All my relatives started crying, but they were tears of happiness. Another special event during the golden anniversary is when the oldest child gives her mother a shawl woven of golden threads. My mother is the oldest daughter, and she sewed a beautiful white silk shawl with golden roses. When everybody was sitting at the anniversary table, my mother approached the "bride" and gently covered her fragile shoulders and kissed her cheeks. It was another moment for tears of joy. All the guests stood up and applauded.

During the party, many good and warm words were given to my grandparents. Everybody had a chance to stand up and say something to the "newlyweds." At the end of their golden wedding ceremony, romantic music was playing. My grandfather took my grandmother's hand very carefully and invited her to dance. All thirty guests stood up from their places and made a big ring around them. After that, my mother gave everybody burning candles, and someone turned off the lights. My grandparents were dancing in the middle of a golden ring. It was a very symbolic, traditional dance of one strong family.

Gifts for wedding anniversaries are another interesting part of our traditions. In my country, there are books with information and recommendations about gifts for each wedding anniversary. According to our tradition, the present should be connected with the material which symbolizes a particular anniversary. Gifts can be jewelry, household appliances, or simple souvenirs. For example, my sister and I gave our parents silver rings for their silver anniversary, and they put their new silver rings on top of their gold wedding rings. Two years ago, they celebrated their pearl anniversary (thirty years). Their friends organized a party for them near a beautiful lake and gave my parents a very interesting traditional gift. They bought thirty pearls and special thread, and placed them in a crystal vase. During the party, my parents assembled a very nice necklace for my mother. It was a symbol of their life together.

This year my husband and I celebrated our first anniversary. He bought me a beautiful bouquet of roses, and we exchanged special chintz handkerchiefs with our names on them. We'll save those chintz handkerchiefs for our golden wedding anniversary.

Celebrating wedding anniversaries each year is a lovely and meaningful tradition for a family. I want to continue this remarkable tradition, and I hope one day, in forty-nine years, my husband and I will celebrate our golden anniversary with our children and grandchildren just as my grandparents did.

## Celebrating in Brazil

EDNA CARVALHO

WHEN A COUPLE DECIDES TO marry, they expect that their marriage will be for the rest of their lives. In my country Brazil, we celebrate this life together beginning with the first year of marriage. However, there are special wedding anniversaries celebrated with bigger parties and ceremonies such as the twenty-fifth, fiftieth, and sixtieth.

The first year of marriage is celebrated with a big party. The couple is happy to be together, and they have many plans to walk side by side. Usually the couple organized the party, and sometimes they invite family and friends to join them. From the second year of marriage to the twenty-fourth, the couple celebrates simply. Many times it is just a dinner together, or the husband surprises his wife with red flowers and expensive jewelry. The twenty-fifth wedding anniversary, however, marks a very important milestone for the couple, and their twenty-five years together are celebrated with a big party. Everyone on both sides of the family as well as friends is invited to be with them. This celebration is called the silver party. On this occasion, the couple rents a place to receive all their guests and decorates it all in silver colors. Sometimes the guests bring expensive gifts such as jewelry, porcelain vases, books, or personal items. At the end of the party, the couple gives a little silver box full of chocolate to every single guest.

Five years ago, I had the chance to attend my aunt's twenty-fifth wedding anniversary, and it was a fantastic silver party. My aunt and her husband rented a club and invited all their family and friends. My grandmother was responsible for the wonderful and varied food, which made everybody very happy. There was one type of food, *creme de galinha,* which everybody especially liked. Besides that, everybody was dressed very elegantly. My aunt wore a long silver dress, and her husband wore a tuxedo. At the end of the party, the couple gave a small silver box full of chocolates to everybody at the party.

The fiftieth year of marriage is celebrated with an even bigger party than the twenty-fifth. The couple's families organize a party and invite friends to join them. This huge event is called the golden party, and all the decorations are in gold colors. When the family is rich, they offer a very fancy dinner and very special drinks. One unique tradition at the gold party is that the woman has to dance with every man in the family. When the family is really big, she might ask to stop dancing because she can't dance all night since she is not a teenager anymore. The family gives a little golden box full of chocolates to each guest, and in exchange, they give very expensive gifts to the couple.

When my grandparents celebrated their own fiftieth wedding anniversary, our family threw a very big gold party. My grandmother danced with all the men in the family: her husband, sons, grandsons, and sons-in-law. At the end of the party, she was really tired but happy to celebrate her life and her long marriage with all those she loved.

Even more special than the twenty-fifth and fiftieth anniversaries is the sixtieth wedding anniversary. This is a rare event because of the couple's age, but when it does happen, the family celebrates with a two-day party. On the first day, there is a religious ceremony where the couple's marriage vows are renewed. Usually each grandchild is responsible for choosing and reading a Bible passage during the religious service. On the second day, there is a party with lots of food and music.

I was lucky to have the unique experience of going to a sixtieth wedding anniversary. My neighbors' wedding anniversary took two days to celebrate, and it was an unforgettable party. On the first night, there was a religious ceremony, and all the children from the couple's family sang in the church. On the second day, the family gave a big party with wonderful food and a great band singing nice music. It was an amazing experience to witness my neighbors celebrating their lives together.

In short, important wedding anniversaries in Brazil are celebrated with beautiful parties, and people love to participate in those celebrations because they are celebrating life.


## My Grandparents' Anniversary
JOSÉ RAMIREZ


IN JALISCO AND MUCH OF the rest of Mexico, we have the tradition of celebrating wedding anniversaries, with the most special being the silver or twenty-fifth, the golden or fiftieth, and the platinum or seventy-fifth. Each of these important anniversaries is celebrated with a mass, often by the same priest who said the couple's wedding mass and in the same church where they were married. The anniversary masses are celebrated so that a couple can renew their wedding vows and thank God for all the years of being together and for the family they have created. After the mass, there is usually a reception with relatives and close friends. There isn't any traditional anniversary food for the reception. The couple may choose Mexican food or something different.

Four years ago my family celebrated the fiftieth anniversary of my paternal grandparents, and we were fortunate to have the same priest and the same church we had had for their twenty-fifth anniversary. It was very special. My grandparents walked down the aisle of the church, my grandmother in a wheelchair and my grandfather with a cane. My grandfather wore a black suit, and my grandmother, holding a bouquet of gardenias, wore a beige gown. As all of their family and friends watched them, the church was alive with happiness for all the years they had been together and for the beautiful and united family they had created. During the mass, there was a lovely orchestra playing.

The only unfortunate part of the celebration was the absence of my father and one of his brothers. My father was working in the United States and my uncle in Kenya at the time. But all the rest of the family celebrated with my grandparents: two sons, four daughters, and twelve grandchildren. My grandparents' closest friends also attended.

After the mass, we hosted a small reception at my

aunt's house because my grandparents wanted an intimate celebration. We cooked many traditional Mexican dishes: *carne con chile, carne a la Mexicana,* and *mole dulce.* All the food was delicious. And of course, a special event in Jalisco wouldn't be complete without a *mariachi* band playing regional Mexican music. Everyone loved the small *mariachi* group we hired. There were six rather than twelve musicians, but they played as if they were a group of fifteen. They were funny as well, imitating many famous Mexican singers. We had a really good time that we will treasure all our lives.

Unfortunately, my grandfather died last year, so we won't be able to celebrate my grandparents' seventy-fifth wedding anniversary. It comforts me to know, though, that memory of their anniversary celebration will last for many generations. I hope these traditions never get lost in my culture because, wherever we are in the world, we can stay connected to our history and beliefs through them.

## An Unforgettable Day
FABIAN SILVA SANCHEZ

*I* WAS JUST A SMALL KID when my grandparents celebrated their fiftieth wedding anniversary. Over their long marriage, they had fifteen children, three of whom died, but that is another story. All of my aunts and uncles spent more than a month planning the anniversary party because they wanted it to be an extra special event for my grandparents.

The party was held near my grandparents' home where there was a huge garden next to a creek. I remember this garden as a magical place with a path that led from their home to a grove of banana trees. In fact, to prepare for the party, my uncle cut back a lot of the lush growth in the garden so that the banana trees surrounded newly opened space for the party.

As my aunts and uncles worked hard on the party preparations, everything for the party began arriving at my grandparents' house. Most of the lovely decorations, fine tablecloths, and beautiful vases came from the USA because most of my family was living there. The colors used for the party were red and white because these colors symbolize love and peace.

As the day of the celebration grew near, my uncles who were living in the USA began arriving in Mexico. I was filled with excitement and happiness to have my family members returning because I hadn't seen them in years. A week before the party, my family began preparing a feast in honor of my grandparents and their long marriage. My uncle, Manuel, butchered a cow for the party, and my mom and aunts cut the beef into pieces and decided what dishes to make with it. I was little at the time, so I didn't help with the food preparation. I did, however, carefully observe what my family was doing. I found it fascinating and disgusting at the same time. I remember how big and fat that cow was and how much delicious food it provided for all the guests at the party.

On the day of the party, all the townspeople assembled in the garden, as did my aunts and uncles from other states in Mexico. Some of these relatives I had never met before, and it was wonderful to be surrounded by so many family members and neighbors. At the end of the celebration, fireworks lit up the sky. All the guests were clapping, and my grandparents were smiling. They were so happy, and I was too. I will never forget that day.

# Poems and Hikes

SARAH NIELSEN

*My* HUSBAND AND I RECENTLY celebrated our tenth wedding anniversary. We don't have any children and none of our family members live near us, so we have had to create our own simple traditions to celebrate the life we have built together.

Each year as our anniversary approaches, I use the *New York Public Library Reference Guide* to look up the traditional gift associated with that particular anniversary. After that, I begin work on an anniversary poem for my husband, using the traditional gift as the theme for the poem. For example, the traditional gift for the fifth wedding anniversary is wood, which inspired the poem below.

anniversary poem number five: wood

i like the sound of wood
the sounds we make as we grow some together
a tree of wonder and delight and dark mystery
a tree of what matters and what stays after we are gone

i like the smell of your hair in the morning
sandalwood on a hot day
a deep sweetness, a hint of dark forest floors

i like the taste of your mouth, warm
the lingering of dark red fruit and oak barrel

i like the image of you become me becoming you
just becoming
the woven branches of a tree in a Chinese garden

i like the feel of your roots taking hold of me
digging deep with a slow, steady pulsing
into the flesh of me

I know I will never be a famous poet, but I enjoy the process of writing something for my husband. It gives me a chance to reflect on my life with Jeff and all the things I love about him. Although most of my anniversary poems are mediocre to awful, they are heartfelt and appreciated by my very sweet and supportive audience of one.

In addition to the poem tradition, Jeff and I plan a long hike for our anniversary every year. Sometimes we hike close to home, and other times we travel a great distance to hike. Either way we both enjoy the comfort, perspective, and beauty that nature can provide when we take time to be fully in the present and open ourselves to awe. In our anniversary wanderings, we have hiked in the Santa Cruz Mountains and along the Lost Coast in Sonoma County. We have seen bear-marked trees on the Pacific Crest Coast Trail in Oregon and the Pygmy Forest near Mendocino where a hundred year old cypress tree can be just two feet tall. We have walked winding sections of the Great Wall in China and steep trails above the Na Pali Coast on the island of Kaua'i.

Our anniversary hiking tradition started with our very first anniversary when we decided to try the Berry Creek Falls Trail in Big Basin Redwood State Park in the Santa Cruz Mountains in California, not knowing at the time that this hike would inspire us to include a connection to nature in our annual celebrations of our life together.

The strenuous and beautiful ten-mile hike on the Berry Creek Falls Trail wound down through redwood forests, lush with ferns and wild orchids, dappled in light and shadow of the kind that must have inspired the Impressionists painters of the early twentieth century. At the bottom of the basin, we felt the cool spray of Berry Creek Falls on our faces and marveled at the strength and beauty of that flowing water.

As we climbed back up out of the basin, we saw two other waterfalls. Navigating the slippery steps carved from rock to the right of Silver Falls, we came across a baby rattlesnake and gingerly stepped around it, reminded that even in her smallest incarnations, nature can be both a giver and taker of life. At Golden Falls, we delighted in the water flecked with gold dust.

When we arrived back at the top of the basin after six hours of hiking, we were tired but content, feeling at one with each other and the forest we had walked through together. We knew in that moment that we had begun a special anniversary tradition, one that we hope to continue even as we grow old together.

# Endings

# Endings

## My Father's Funeral

CHUKWUEMEKAM NGENE

*T*HE KINGDOM OF ATTAWU IS in Akgebe Ugwu, Okunano, a town situated just south of Enugu in eastern Nigeria in West Africa. There, life is celebrated from conception to burial with unique traditions at each step along the way. The funeral ceremonies after a loved one dies are of utmost significance there.

When a child is born into my family, the parents rigidly instill a concept of responsibility. They teach that life is about what you leave behind, your name, the family name, and what you make of it. The aim is to perpetuate the name and leave it greater by doing good works. Children learn at a young age that those who bring shame to their fatherland are not buried at home; some are either thrown to the scavengers, *udene*, or buried in shallow graves in the wild forests where beasts might easily exhume and feast upon them. However, when one has lived a good life, honorably, and done things that benefit society, death is celebrated, and the person's place in the communal memory is assured.

A good example of that was my father, Pa Ruben Agbpwp Ngenchingwu. He lived an honorable life and contributed to the lives of others. He saw the coming of the missionaries as God's intervention in our society and embraced the Christian church even when it was a crime to do so. My father lead the campaign to educate everyone, so he sent his children to school and made sure everyone in the family benefited from education. Although he was sometimes misunderstood, he never relinquished the struggle to do what he thought was right. He won the hearts of a few, which ignited enthusiasm in the minds of many. Before his death on January 3, 1999, he touched the lives of many people in a most positive manner. His funeral is a typical example of how a loved one's life is celebrated in my hometown.

When a great man like my father passes on, his first-born child, male or female, is contacted immediately. I was seven hundred miles away from home when my father died. While his body was being taken care of by relatives, I was on my way home from Lagos. Upon arrival, I had a meeting with my sisters and brother. We deliberated on the style, components, and magnitude of our father's funeral. My sisters wanted a strictly Christian burial; however, my brother and I wanted a traditional aspect to it because our father, *Su-ke-emee*, was a titled chief, and he merited that respect. The traditional rites would safeguard our royal status and also accord our family the full recognition and nobility bestowed on the children who give their deserving parents a befitting burial. We agreed to combine these two traditions to honor my father's desire to recognize his Christian faith and also to perpetuate the tradition of our forefathers.

We met with the elders of our village to inquire about the requirements of a traditional ceremony and to tell them our wishes. We chose to give our father a full traditional burial with his titles and the nobility of his kingdom intact. I, as the oldest surviving son, decided where in our family compound our father would be buried.

Preparations began immediately. The young people cut the grass and prepared the area for the grave. Then they dug the grave. As they worked, musicians and dancers encouraged them. On the night before the funeral, a flutist played a tune that invited the living to close their doors and go to bed as the souls of our forefathers were being called forth. The sound could send chills and fear through the veins of everyone, especially the uninitiated, who scrambled for cover. *Achikwu* would come up at midnight with her steady but fearful rhythm. *Okpoko* instrumentation is recognized in my home as the voice of our forefathers. The soulful tunes chronicle the achievements of the dead and describe what he left behind. The heirs are admonished to live up to the good family names and let the torch being handed over to them shine ever brighter.

Through the night, houses for the next day's masquerade were built with palm fronds. The grounds were leveled and prepared for both the dancers and the spectators. My father's funeral day began as tradition demanded. My eldest sister, dressed in my father's royal attire, greeted guests. My younger brother and I dressed in warrior costumes and carried loaded guns. My brother was dressed as a tiger, and I wore lion skins with a bow and arrow. We ran a great distance, which was determined by our elders according to their assessment of our health and courage. We ran the course seven times, demonstrating our bravery and dexterity. That tiring challenge took two hours, in which love for each other and the spirit of teamwork were also tested as we made our way through the obstacles. However, we felt encouraged by relatives and spectators watching from a distance. With each challenge we overcame, we were applauded and the crowd joined in singing praise. When we finally reached our destination, we fired our guns.

After that accomplishment, we were ready for the initiation into the cult of elders, which is reserved only for those who have buried their fathers with honor. Finally, we danced to *Igede* music, which officially announced that we had done well for our father. That session concluded after we offered the required sacrifices which included five traditional domestic animals: cows, goats, dogs, sheep, and slaves. Money was accepted in place of human slaves because they believe that money is the closest thing in modern times that could buy the services that slaves provided in the past.

Once the official tribal initiation ceremonies were over, the festivities began. Various dance groups were invited to perform and each represented an aspect of our tradition. The first was *egwu umunwanyi*, the Women's Dance. The women dressed in colorful velvet clothes and adorned their arms and legs with expensive beads made of elephant tusks and cowries, brightly colored shells, and gold and diamond trinkets. They looked really sexy and inviting as they danced a beautiful and captivating dance. Their glamorous dance included recognition of the importance of mothers in the family.

Another dance is for both men and women. It resembles calisthenics and American break-dancing. *Okanga* is a dance for the youth and middle-aged men only. Their masquerades are colorful, and the amazing dance dramatizes life in the spiritual realm. *Ogene* is for the older boys, the strong and the brave, and has a hard-hitting rhythm. The music can inspire them to do extraordinary things, like climb a tree with their bare hands. Finally comes the *Igede*, with another group of dancers and special music. This is the farewell dance for the soul of the dead and a welcome rhythm to the men he left behind. The dance marks a great accomplishment as only the great and wealthy can meet the demands of this dance.

At sundown, the rest of the dance group came out in full swing in beautiful colors and masquerades. The celebration continued until dusk when visitors went to the homes in our neighborhood to eat and drink. The occasion was brought to an end with the flutist at night calling on the souls of our forefathers to take care of the new soul, my father's. The flute also calls on the departed souls to strengthen those left behind to multiply the good works of the departed by doing the same for others.

## Thai Funeral Ceremony
WANNA

My mother passed away more than four years ago; however, my memories of her death are still as fresh and clear as if it were yesterday. On Friday morning, March 4, 2005, while I was standing next to my mother's bed at the hospital and holding her hand, I noticed that her breathing had changed dramatically. A few moments later, the nurse came toward me and told me that it was time for her to go. My heart was breaking, and my body was shaking. I collapsed on the chair and tears flooded my eyes, but no sound of crying came out of me. The moment of her death, the end of her dear life, also meant the beginning of my planning for her funeral.

Although I had just lost my mother, I had no time for grieving then. I had so many things to do in order to take her remains back to our hometown in the south of Thailand and prepare for the rituals and ceremony for her death.

As we are Thai Buddhists, we begin with the bathing ceremony. The immediate family, relatives, and friends pour water over the hands of the deceased to symbolize an apology for any wrongs committed to the deceased during life. This is also a time to say good-bye for the last time, and to bless the spirit for the journey to the place of peace. The bathing ceremony takes place at the same location where the whole funeral ceremony takes place. The family can choose to have the ceremony at home or at the temple. After the bathing ceremony, members of the immediate family or relatives, normally men, dress the deceased in the clothes that the family has chosen. Then the deceased is placed in the coffin. The coffin always faces west because Thai Buddhists believe that the west is the symbol of the ending, and the east is the symbol of the beginning. Family members decorate the coffin with wreaths, flowers, candles, and sticks of incense, and they place a photograph of the deceased alongside the coffin. People who live in the city normally have the ceremony at the temple because it is convenient. People who live in the countryside, on the other hand, normally arrange for the ceremony at their home. In my mother's case, we chose to have the ceremony at our home.

Thai Buddhism relies on monks, so they schedule the date of the ceremony. The funeral ceremony takes three, five, or seven days depending on the family. However, they will not cremate the deceased on a Wednesday because they believe that if cremation takes place on that day it will bring bad luck or death to the rest of family who are still alive. For example, if the family wants to cremate within three days and the third day is on Wednesday, then they have to postpone it for one day or two days or longer depending on the family's decision. In my mother's case, we decided to have the ceremony for seven days, so our relatives who live in different provinces could attend the ceremony and pay their last respects to my mother.

During the funeral ceremonies, at a home or at a temple, family members and guests dress in black, white, or dark clothes. From the first to the last day, monks come during the evening prayer time to chant prayers. Also, friends and neighbors gather in the evening for a feast and a prayer ceremony.

On the last day of the funeral ceremony, when the funeral takes place at home, the monks come to chant and pray. Then the leader of the monks carries a white banner, which is connected to the coffin. Next, the men move the coffin into a special car, and the procession travels to the cemetery located at the temple. When the procession arrives at the cemetery, they place the coffin in the cremation chamber. Monks chant for the last time, and then they toss the torches and incense on to the fragrant flower wood beneath the coffin. Then the guests and relatives go back to their homes. It is now time for the family who lost their loved one to be by themselves at the temple. I remember sitting on the bench looking at the smoke in the sky and crying. It was the first time that I allowed myself time for grieving.

Early the next morning after the cremation, the family goes back to the cemetery to collect the ashes that were put into the urn by a monk. They either leave the urn at the temple or bring it home depending on the family's belief. In my mother's case, we left her urn at the temple cemetery. Once the urn is at the temple, the family often goes to the temple to pay respect.

After the funeral ceremony, family members may wear white or black clothes for a period of time, such as a month or one hundred days, to show that they are mourning their loved one. Family members will also gather to pay respect to their loved one on the hundredth day after their death. Some families also gather to pay respect once a year, often on the same date that the person died. This annual celebration depends on the family situation. For example, although I am living in the United States now, I try to go back to my hometown to join my family for this ceremony.

## Burial in Mexico

BRENDA PINEDA

WHEN SOMEONE IN A FAMILY dies, it is very difficult and sad for those still living to be without the loved one who has been important in life. When death separates us from a loved one, we celebrate the life of the one who died. Many religions teach that the death is not the end of life but the beginning of the spiritual life. In my native country, Mexico, many people practice Catholicism, which also teaches that our souls live on in eternity. In Mexico, many people are also Guadalupanos, those who have faith in the Virgin of Guadalupe. This combination of beliefs results in some unique burial customs in Mexico.

The first day after someone dies is call *velorio*, which means that the body is veiled for a day. Many years ago, people believed that the body should be veiled for three days, but my grandmother told me that the government decided that it was not healthy. This one-day *velorio* offers the family and friends of the deceased the opportunity to view the body for the last time. Before the viewing, the body is prepared by family members, who dress the deceased in his or her favorite clothes. Children are always dressed in white. Then the body is placed inside the metal or wooden casket. After that, the *velorio* begins. The family, friends, and neighbors view the deceased for one last time and offer their good-byes. They also express condolences and comfort to the family that suffered the loss. In my family, the death of my grandmother, Luisa, was very difficult, but many friends honored her and were with us to provide support. The friends and neighbors came to my grandmother's house when they learned of her death. They brought candles and flowers to put around the casket of my grandmother. Her daughters had dressed her in jeans, a cute shirt, and pumps because these were her favorite clothes. During the *velorio*, we stayed awake all night and people prayed around her casket to her spirit.

The second day is a day of great emotions and sadness. This is *el entierro*. The body is brought to the church for the funeral mass and then to the cemetery for burial. The family members carry the casket from the church to the cemetery. When we buried my grandmother, all of her friends, our friends, and our relatives walked with us from the church to the cemetery. They carried flowers and played music along the way. At the gravesite, someone lit fireworks. This kind of support seems like a party, but in many towns in Mexico it demonstrates support and respect for this difficult situation. When the burial of my grandmother concluded, everyone went to her house and ate food with us. This was a great support and comfort to my family.

The day of the burial is not the end of the funeral services. The next nine days are *novenario*. Every day for nine days, family members and those who loved the deceased pray the rosary to the Virgin of Guadalupe together in the family's home. Each day the family serves coffee and bread to the people who pray the rosary. In many cases, friends bring the bread and coffee to support the family. The last day of *novenario*, the family and friends take a cross made of metal or wood to the cemetery and put this at the place where the body rests, and there the family gives thanks to the people who supported them during the difficult times. I remember that on the last day of the *novenario* of my grandma my family gave thanks to all the people who went to my grandparents' house every night to pray for my grandmother.

In Mexico, *velorio*, *el entierro*, and *novenario* provide the opportunity to comfort and cry together when a loved one dies. These unique funeral services create an opportunity for friends and family to share the loss and take care of each other during a sad and difficult time.

## The Final Celebration

KIM

CELEBRATIONS OF LIFE BEGIN WITH birth and continue throughout childhood and adulthood with birthdays, graduations, weddings, anniversaries, and finally funerals.

While people celebrate throughout their lives, sometimes with annual celebrations, a funeral is a one-time event. It marks the end of life and a farewell to a loved one.

I have been to funerals in both Korea and the United States. My father, my father-in-law, and my aunt have all died. In America, I have attended two funerals. One was the father of my son's friend; the other was the son of my husband's friend. The young man was a Marine who died in Iraq. He was only twenty-one years old. Funerals are similar in Korea and the United States in that people grieve for the loss of a loved one. The way people in each culture do that, however, is not always so similar.

I had a very special experience at my grandfather-in-law's funeral. The funeral was held in traditional Korean style. I had seen this type of funeral in movies, but had never experienced one. My grandfather-in-law died at his home in the countryside in Korea. I had met him only once before he died, just six months after our wedding. He did not attend the wedding because he was suffering from Alzheimer's disease. My grandfather-in-law had two sons and five daughters. My husband is the first son of the first son. In Korean tradition, the first son has the responsibility for arranging family events, including funerals.

When my husband's grandfather died, his body was prepared in a traditional manner. First, his body was washed and a *suwie*, a shroud, was wrapped around of him, and his body was put in a casket placed inside of his room. We used a beautiful traditional eight-piece screen to conceal his casket. In front of the casket, a long table held an incense burner, rice, rice wine, dried pollock, and fruits. Flowers were placed on the left and right sides of the table. Rice was chosen because it has long been the most important grain in Korea.

At the funeral ceremony, the family wore traditional unbleached clothes, and everyone wore shoes called *zipsin*, made of braided straw. My father-in-law and my husband stood at the front of the room where each guest first bowed to them then bowed to the casket, kneeling with their hands and head almost on the floor. Then they got up and made sorrowful sounds together like chanting for the deceased. After this, each guest lit incense and bowed twice more in front of the casket. His funeral lasted for three days. While men welcomed the guests, women, including me, prepared food for the family, guests, and townspeople. We steamed pork, cooked rice, and made a lot of different vegetables for side dishes. For each meal, we prepared food for my deceased grandfather-in-law. We presented the food, bowing before his casket and making mournful sounds together. Then we took our own meal. The neighbors and friends from the whole town helped us. It was like a town party, without the music and dancing.

On the third day, pallbearers were chosen. They brought in the casket carrier beautifully decorated with pink, yellow, white, blue, and green flowers. It did not look like a casket carrier to me, but it was. After breakfast, the entire family made one last bow and mournful chant together. Finally, the pallbearers put the casket on the casket carrier and started to move the casket. It looked like they used all their strength, but the casket did not move. I still cannot tell whether it was the carriers or my grandfather-in-law who did not want to leave his house, but the casket would not move. Then we prepared food and rice wine in front of the casket, and my father-in-law told his father how much we loved him, but that we had to let him go, that he should not worry about us but just rest his body and soul in heaven. Then the pallbearers ate and drank and afterward easily carried the casket from the house. They stopped at several of my grandfather-in-law's favorite places along the way, and at each one, the pallbearers stood in front of the casket; they bowed, offered rice wine and food just as they had done at home. Finally, we reached the family graveyard. There, the casket was placed in the grave, which was dug by the young men in town. The first son threw soil and a flower into the grave and said in Korean, "Peace to your soul in heaven." Then the funeral ended. He was born from a human body, but he was buried in the earth. After the funeral, women wore a little white bow tie pin in their hair, and men wore a little white bow on their chest for about a month.

My grandfather-in-law's funeral was twenty-five years ago, but I still remember everything about it. I have also held memorial services for him here in America. In traditional Korea culture, most people celebrate their ancestor's memorial day for at least three generations. He died on September 21, 1984, on the lunar calendar, which was November 7, on the solar calendar. According to our tradition, I prepare traditional food for his memorial day. When I cook this food, I do not use spices, and I prepare a number of dishes and set up a table according to the traditional rules. Then before midnight, we open the front door, which symbolizes a welcome. We light incense, pour rice wine, and bow to him, my ancestor's spirits. We do not worship them; we only show our respect to them even though they are dead. We tell our children how much great-grandfather, whom they have never met, loved their dad. This custom will end when I am gone because my children are too Americanized to understand it. Until then, I will keep my country's traditional custom.

# Praise at the End

ANONYMOUS

*In the middle of a* silent night, some bells ring throughout the town, signifying someone traveling on the final journey. In my native country, Japan, a funeral is conducted in a serious and silent manner. I have a particularly strong memory of my grandfather's death and funeral.

I was fifteen years old when I learned that my seventy-five year old grandfather on my father's side had passed away. My family, my parents, younger sister, older brother and I quickly traveled to his house by train. We brought appropriate black clothes before we left. At my grandparent's house, I saw many people. About a third of them were my relatives, and the rest were my grandfather's friends. I met many relatives for the first time.

As the sun was setting into the horizon, we walked to the temple that my grandfather had attended throughout his life, beginning in his youth. The temple looked old and dignified. We walked around the outside and then into the temple to see where the funeral would be conducted. Inside the temple, in the center of a room, I saw the long wooden box that held my grandfather. Through the little window, I could see his face, which looked comfortable, but I could not see all of him. Throughout the evening until midnight, my grandfather's friends and I talked about whatever seemed interesting but not related to the funeral. I met one of my grandfather's friends who lived at the bottom of a mountain and worked for a traditional Japanese sweets and snacks company. While we were talking, I noticed that the food for the funeral service had been made by this man's company, and I was suddenly filled with appreciation for him.

The next day at sunrise, many people, dressed neatly in black, came to the temple. One of the monks, who was about sixty years old, silently entered the temple, and suddenly I could not hear any noise. Silence shrouded the temple. Soon, each visitor walked to the casket and bowed in front of my grandfather. They placed an incense stick in the incense holder, put their hands together, walked back a little and finally bowed deeply again. The monk started to read aloud from the Buddhist scriptures. No one knew what he said exactly, but some people could understand the general meaning of the scriptures. The funeral continued for about three hours. Then we all went back to my grandparents' house, and the monk started to read the scriptures again. We repeated this process several times throughout the day. At sunset, my entire family went to the crematorium, which made us deeply sad. My grandmother could not stop crying, and we all grieved for her as well as for my grandfather. She was the only one who saw my grandfather turned into the white bones and ashes at the crematorium. Finally, we placed my grandfather's remains in the ground.

After the funeral, we all went to a restaurant that my grandfather especially liked. There was no seriousness in the restaurant. We talked as we had before the funeral with simple, pleasant everyday conversation and ate some dishes of sushi. Later, I read some letters that people had written to him and realized that a person's life should not simply be defined by what he or she has done but also by how others feel about the person and how they praise that life. As I was reading those letters, tears began to flow down my face. Suddenly, I knew my grandfather and my loss.

# Stunning Funerals

JENNY

TAIWAN ALLOWS CITIZENS TO PRACTICE any religion they like, but most people practice Buddhism or Taoism, a Chinese philosophy based on the writings of Lao-Tzu. Each of these religions teaches the same strong belief in reincarnation and in expecting the next life to be better after they die. My family's religion is a mixture of Buddhism and Taoism. That means we worship the gods of both religions. These special beliefs have influenced my family to have unique funeral ceremonies when someone passes away.

I remember that when I was thirty years old, I attended my grandfather's funeral in my hometown of Gia-ee. He died of brain cancer at the age of ninety-seven. His body lay in a coffin over dry ice under a temperate shed in the front yard of his house for forty-nine days, which is the minimum required for a dead person to complete his or her reincarnation according to Buddhist theory. During the forty-nine days, my family hired Buddhist monks to pray at home for my grandfather and expected that this would allow him to have a better reincarnation. We also hired actors and actresses to perform traditional Taiwanese operas in the front yard to entertain my dead grandfather, the neighbors, and our visitors. We created wreaths with red colored paper as decorations. The whole funeral ceremony was like a happy party because we believe that when people live beyond the age of eighty, they are lucky, and that the family should celebrate their achievement of a long life by using red colored paper, not just the usual white and black, to show that good luck.

Then on the forty-ninth day, the last day, all the family members walked around the coffin, touched his face, and took the unbearable last glance at him before we closed the coffin. For the funeral procession, we hired professional criers to help us cry loudly in order to show our family members' deep and sincere mourning. Before we put dirt on the coffin, we also hired Taoist monks to pray for him because we believe that different religious gods could help my grandfather have a better chance for a good reincarnation. After the burial, we held a big party at home, offering all the visitors a feast with food and drink, and everybody seemed to feel better and not be so sad.

In contrast, when I attended my niece's funeral, the situation was totally different. My niece died in a car accident at the age of nineteen. Her funeral ceremony was simple and full of sadness. Her body did not lie in the coffin at home for forty-nine days but was put in a freezer at the crematorium for a few days. Her parents only hired one Taoist monk to pray for her in the cremation rites and brought sticks to beat her coffin and scolded her before having her cremated. In addition, her parents and elder family members were not allowed to watch her body being cremated, only her brothers and sisters were allowed to watch the cremation, collect her cremains, and put them in an urn. Later, this urn was placed in a small Buddhist temple, and only the siblings were allowed to pray for her because if any of her elder relatives or parents prayed for her that would cause her to have a bad reincarnation. After the funeral ceremony, her parents invited the guests to have a simple lunch and led them to another Taoist temple and paid a monk to pray for us in order to help us get rid of evil spirits touching us during the funeral ceremony. Additionally, her parents and elder relatives were allowed to visit the Buddhist temple to show their grief and care for her for only one year. The reason we do this is to punish the dead young child for not taking care of her parents when her parents are old. This also allows the dead child to forget her parents and relatives of this life and to go quickly on to her next life.

Taiwanese people respect those who have a long life but disrespect those who die young because according to Buddhist theory, one who has a long life must have done many good things in his or her last life, but one who has a short life must have committed some crimes or committed suicide in his or her last life. By comparing these two funerals, I understand how precious life is and that people should try their best to have a long good life and devote themselves to help the world if they wish to have a ceremonious funeral and a better reincarnation after they die.

## My Father's Death

MINOO SHAGHAFI

IN LIFE WE HAVE MANY choices, but we cannot make choices about our birth or our death. Death is a part of life that brings sadness in all cultures. In Persian culture, in Iran, when someone dies, the first forty days are very important. When my father died, I was a teenager, but I still remember that day very clearly. I also remember his funeral.

My father was a lovely parent; he had a beautiful smile and a strong personality. He never complained about anything. Instead, he found solutions and offered good advice. He had a healthy, useful, and productive life. He usually spent his free time reading books and newspapers or listening to the news. He also paid a lot of attention to his nutrition. He ate healthy foods, especially fruits and vegetables, and exercised daily. He never got sick and was never on medication or in the hospital until one week before his death. Suddenly, on a cloudy and rainy day in November, when I came home from school, he was lying on his bed. It seemed unusual, so I was worried about him. I felt something was wrong, outside of our usual daily routine. Unfortunately, I was right. He called my older brother who was visiting from the United States and me into his room and told us that he had pain in his chest and upper left side. My brother immediately called emergency services. They sent an ambulance and transferred him to the hospital. Unfortunately, he had a heart attack at home, and the next day in the hospital he had a stroke. He died five days later. This was such a shock to us because he had always been in good health, and he took good care of himself.

We planned a huge funeral for him. This included a ceremony on the third day, the seventh day, and the fortieth day after his death, as is the tradition in our culture. In Iran when someone dies, his or her family and relatives gather in a spiritual ceremony. We pray, share our sadness, show respect for the departed, eat special foods, and spend time together. At my father's ceremony, our house was filled with white flowers and black ribbons. His picture adorned the wall. This is a common practice. In Iran white candles are a symbol of happiness, and we usually light a white candle at weddings. For a funeral, we light a black candle as a symbol of sadness. On the seventh day after someone dies, we visit the cemetery, bring food and flowers, and say prayers. Forty days later, we do the same thing. We visit the cemetery, bring food and flowers, and say prayers. During this time the family wears black clothes, and they do not join any parties or celebrations. In some families, relatives wear black clothes for a year.

I remember when my father passed away. Now many years later, I can still see his face in my mind and appreciate his beliefs and wisdom.

## The Day of the Dead

MARIA VEGA DE TOVAR

ONE OF THE OLDEST AND most significant celebrations in Mexico is the Day of the Dead. This is a special time when we celebrate the lives of loved ones who have died. All across the country people follow old customs with altars and special rituals at home and at the cemetery. The most beautiful aspects of the Day of the Dead are the altars, the rituals, and the celebrations for our loved ones who have passed away.

Families celebrate the lives of their deceased relatives at home by making an altar. They place a framed picture of that person on a large table with a white tablecloth. On the table, they place a vase of *cempasuchil*, beautiful flowers that the Aztecs used to remember their dead. People also put two kinds of small sugar figurines that allude to death on the table. People can make or buy these colorful skull or complete skeleton figurines that have names of the deceased written on the forehead. Other types of figurines are small dolls, which have tall thin bodies, beautiful dresses, and skull heads. Those are called *katrina*, which means an elegant well dressed person. *Katrinas* are usually made of *papier-mache*, but you can find them also made of sugar or wood. The table has the favorite food of the people in the pictures. The family takes great care in preparing all of the food and favorite beverages just as the deceased person liked them. The table also has the very popular Day of the Dead bread, which is adorned with strips of dough simulating bones.

Families also celebrate at the cemetery on November Second. In the morning, people go to the cemetery to clean the tombs and adorn them with a lot of flowers like roses, white lilies, and carnations, but especially with *cempasuchil*. In the evening, people have a picnic with the souls of their deceased relatives. They take all the food from the home altar to the cemetery where we presume that the souls have returned to earth. The people celebrate with songs and prayers that are elevated to the sky for the eternal rest of the souls, even though it is cold at night some people sleep in the cemeteries. This is a festive occasion with music and family and friends.

In addition to these celebrations close to home, many people from different parts of the country travel to the state of Michoacán to the small city of Patzcuaro. The people there celebrate this tradition on November 2 every year in a most fantastic manner, and people want to see the ritual of the Day of the Dead. This custom is one of the most amazing in the entire country. Patzcuaro is a beautiful city with a small island, Janitzio, in the middle of the Patzcuaro Lake. All along the pier are good restaurants with typical food and appetizers and shops full of native handmade art such as baskets, wooden toys, tablecloths, jewelry, and much more. The families and friends begin the celebration during the day, and they wait until midnight to see the ritual. They have to wear warm clothes because the climate is cold and windy, but people sell hot drinks all along the pier. By the time the ritual begins, people are standing close to the lake to see the wonderful scene with the moon reflected on the water and all the candles that people light and put into small canoes. Some of the candles are just on a piece of wood that floats on the lake. At the same time, fisherman are standing in their canoes in the middle of the lake, dancing the butterfly ritual. They are moving butterfly nets with their arms. All this is because the families believe that the soul of the dead will come down to the earth to celebrate with their love ones, and the light of those candles floating on the lake will guide the souls on their way. At the magic moment, the moon's rays fall onto the lake like a waterfall. Many people think that those rays are the souls or spirits from the dead people.

When we remember the dead, we have in mind sadness, sorrows, chills, and maybe pain. But when Mexican people think about the Day of the Dead, they think of a big celebration where our most important guests are our loved ones, our deceased relatives. This tradition provides one of the most colorful, happy, and unforgettable days of the year.

## Día de los Muertos
NANCY Z. HERNANDEZ

DIA DE LOS MUERTOS IS a beautiful traditional Catholic event celebrated by Mexican families every year on November 2 to honor to our loved ones who passed away. This is a celebration where a special altar is set up, a mass is offered for the dead, and lots of delicious food is prepared and shared with everyone. This is a day when we expose our deepest feelings of both sadness and happiness, but is also the time when all the family is reunited to comfort each other.

Before the holiday, we prepare all the decorations for the altar. The altar is usually made of wood or boxes, and it looks like a pyramid with three levels. The bottom part represents earth, the middle one represents death, and the top represents heaven. This altar can be set up at different places. If we can't be at the cemetery because the graveside of our loved one is far away from where we live, it can be at home or at church, for all the souls. If we live near the cemetery, the altar is at the graveside of our deceased loved ones. I remember when my mom, my grandmother, and I made flowers in different bright colored tissue paper. The colors each symbolized something: pink representing celebration, yellow representing death, purple representing pain, and white representing hope. We used the flowers to make wreaths in the shape of a cross for my grandfather who passed away many years ago. Also we made some *papel picado*, punched paper banners. The same kind of paper is put at the top of the altar to represent the sky. This is beautiful Mexican art that was created by the Aztecs. We draw and cut out simple or elaborate patterns or design happy skeletons, crosses, letters and more. After we finished the paper decorations, my entire family helped with the decoration of the candles. We used colorful glitter to draw pictures and write the names of people who are deceased. Then we cooked all the food, *tamales*, *pozole*, *birria*, and *mole* that would be shared later on.

Then we all went to the cemetery around 7:00 am, taking all the food and decorations, plus some fresh aromatic orange flowers called *cempasuchil*, marigold. At the cemetery, we cleaned and decorated the gravesides of our family members and friends. The decorations included a cross made of flowers, the fresh *cempasuchil*, flowers, wreaths, pictures of the deceased, toys, some sugar skulls, a variety of food and drinks like hot chocolate, sodas, *tequila*, or tea, and candles to illuminate the way for the souls. These offerings are things that the deceased enjoyed in life. They can consume the food and drink during the day after the family goes home to prepare for the later celebrations. My grandfather used to drink too much *tequila* and liked *mole*, and we always brought these offerings to him.

After all the preparation of the altar, my whole family and I used to go to the church at the cemetery, where we celebrated a mass of remembrance of all our loved ones whom we keep in our hearts and minds. At church, everyone was invited to place his or her own decorations on the altar. This structure of three levels was covered with a white fabric. On top, right in the middle was the most important piece for Catholic people, the cross where Jesus was crucified. Around the top we placed the *papel picado*, and the rest of the space was full of statues, sugar skulls, and pictures of the deceased people. The altar had colorful flowers, especially *cempasuchil*, different dishes and drinks like *tamales*, *mole*, *enchiladas*, *tequila*, sodas, hot chocolate, *atole*, coffee and much more. We could smell the amazing combination of aromas throughout the church. Everyone, including young children, older boys and girls, men and women, lit candles. This is to honor all the souls. A priest celebrated the mass, and talked about death to help us prepare ourselves for death. We prayed and sang to God for guidance and compassion. After mass, we finally went back to the cemetery where my mom, grandma, aunts, and our entire family, gathered together. We sat together around the grave. We drank coffee, *tequila*, or *atole* and ate the *pozole*, *tamales*, and *mole*. This was the time to share the food, drinks, and affection. When night came, we shared special anecdotes about our family.

On this special holiday, we remember what our loved ones enjoyed most and what they did in life. It is a time when families are reunited again. We cry, laugh, and remember. We prepare the altar together, enjoy the food together, and attend mass together to honor and remember those whose life on earth has ended. This is a sad time because physically our loved ones are no longer with us. But we are sure they are now resting with Our Lord. Remembering keeps them alive.

CHAPTER EIGHT

# Quiet Inspirations

# Quiet Inspirations

## My Childhood Idol

OLIVERA PANIC

LIKE MANY CHILDREN, I HAD a childhood idol, a favorite person whom I adored. He continued to be my idol throughout my childhood and into my adult life. He was not my idol alone; he was the idol of many people because of his life as a doctor. He was the most interesting person I have met so far, and many of his students say the same thing. In Serbia, he was famous for saving many lives during his long career as a doctor. After he passed away in November 1999, the government of the city where he lived and worked decided to rename the main street after him. The street is now Dr. Radoslav Milojevic-Raja. Dr. Raja was the best surgeon in Yugoslavia, and one of the best professors at the Medical University in Belgrade, but for me he was the best grandpa in the world. Many people know about my grandpa, but just a few of us know his wondrous life story.

My mother, my grandmother, and my grandfather have all told me interesting stories about his experience in World War II, his career, and the love of his life.

When he was young, my grandpa never dreamed of becoming a doctor. As a teenager, he wanted to become a priest at the local church. At that time, singing was an important part of the priesthood, and he couldn't sing well. His application was rejected. He was very disappointed at first, but then my grandpa joined the Royal Academy of Yugoslavia. After two years of army education and training, World War II began. My grandpa was sent to war. He battled in Germany against German Nazis, and after a year they captured my grandpa's troop. He spent the rest of the war in a German prison. While he was in prison, he started to read books about human anatomy and medicine. Fortunately, he could read Latin. These were the only books available to him because he could not read German, but he could read Latin. He used this new knowledge to help sick prisoners, and eventually he actually performed surgery in the prison. He became the prison doctor. Soon after that he was treating German soldiers as well. My grandpa told me many stories about the war and his life in prison, but one holds a special place in my memory. It is about a young German soldier who was brought to the hospital almost dead. He had lost a lot of blood because his stomach and his legs were badly injured during a bombing. Everyone, including the soldier himself, thought that he would be dead by sunrise. Not my grandpa! He spent all night treating the soldier's wounds. Alone and determined, he succeeded. He saved the soldier's life and his legs. Grandpa told me that he prayed for that soldier's life all night. Even though the soldier was his enemy, his country's enemy, and he was a soldier in the army that captured him and held him prisoner, my grandpa wanted the soldier to live. That German solider was one of hundreds of people whom my grandpa saved. He never asked if the patient was a good person or not. His duty was to save lives, and he did that very well.

After three long years in the German prison, my grandpa was free again. The war was finally over, and all the prisoners were sent back home. Then my grandpa attended the Medical University of Yugoslavia. He became a brilliant student and medical assistant. Many other students and even doctors came to learn from his war experiences. Before his thirtieth birthday, my grandpa had a medical degree. He finally became an official doctor. Grandpa was soon a well-known young doctor, and the best hospitals wanted to employ him. He chose to work at all of them, and so he traveled to hospitals around Yugoslavia. He was a specialist for the most difficult surgeries, and sometimes he traveled in a helicopter for emergency cases. During those years, he made many friends all over our country.

In 1950, a team of German doctors invited my grandpa to the hospital and Medical University of Berlin. Even though the Yugoslavian government didn't like the idea, my grandpa accepted the invitation. The Germans praised him in a speech and expressed their appreciation for his service. They also gave him a medal for saving the soldier's life. Many people expressed their appreciation in letters, and my family still has these letters as a memory of grandpa's work. He read the Hippocratic Oath in one of those books in the German prison. This is an ancient oath that doctors have taken for many hundreds of years. New doctors all over the world still take this oath. They promise to respect their patients, to practice the art of medicine, to prevent disease, to honor their fellow human beings, and to experience the joy of healing. Thus, he associated that oath in a positive way with his experience in Germany. My grandpa always followed the Hippocratic Oath, no matter who the patient was.

Indeed, I learned from him to care about people no matter where they are from. Thanks to him and his beliefs, today I have friends from all around the world, from Africa, America, and Europe, from Ukraine, China and Australia. I learned from my grandpa that we are all human beings deserving human respect.

In addition to being a dedicated doctor, my grandpa was a handsome man, tall and fit with beautiful blue eyes and black-gray hair. He got gray hair very young. My grandmother told me that before she met my grandpa, she heard many stories about him. She heard that he had one girlfriend in each hospital, usually young pretty nurses, but my grandpa never admitted it. One time I asked him about his love life, and he told me a romantic story. He said that he met the most beautiful girl he'd ever seen in one of his anatomy classes. As a professor, he was not allowed to become close with his students. For the whole semester, he was secretly looking at the beautiful student, and in the end, my grandpa was in love. Unfortunately, when the semester was over, he moved back to the city where he was born to open a new hospital. He thought about her often for a long time, and when he had lost hope of ever seeing her again, they met. She was a young pediatrician in the new hospital. They were from the same city. In the beginning, she was afraid of the handsome, famous doctor and his reputation, but after a while she fell in love with him. They got married in 1954, and after a year my mom was born. My grandparents spent their lives working at the same hospital, teaching at the Medical University, taking good care of their patients, and taking care of their two children. When I was born, both of them were retired, but my grandpa was still a special professor at the university. My grandparents took care of me every summer. We went to many fun places, and wherever we went, people greeted us with love. When I was about fifteen years old, my grandma got diabetes. The sickness slowed her down. All of us, including my grandpa, took good care of her. After she passed away in July 1999, my grandpa's heart was broken. Shortly after that, in November of the same year, his heart stopped. He died of sadness. That year was very sad for our family, and for many people who loved my grandparents.

My grandparents influenced many people in their careers. They practiced the art of medicine and taught many medical students who have continued to keep the spirit of my grandparents alive through their own practice. My grandparents also had a big influence on my decision to become a teacher of special needs children. From them, I also learned to believe in love and marriage. Every time I visit my mom, I proudly walk down the street of Dr. Radoslav Milojevic-Raja and think about his unusual life.

My grandparents were good people from whom I learned to love people equally. My grandpa was an idol and a role model for many other doctors. My goal is to become a teacher for special needs children, and that is how the lives of my grandparents have influenced me. As my grandpa learned to be a doctor in a foreign country, I am studying to be a teacher far away from home. He was the hero of my childhood. I think about him and his life often, and he is still my best teacher and idol.

# An Inspiration

JENNY

*I* REMEMBER MY GRANDMOTHER AS AN intelligent, tall, and strong woman who always offered all her grandchildren free movie tickets and free sweet treats when we visited her. She was illiterate because she came from a poor farm family and never had the chance to go to school. Unbelievably, my father's family depended on her business skills to survive after World War II. Her life was like a great epic that has inspired me. She showed through example the courage and tolerance of traditional Taiwanese women.

When she was thirteen years old, she obeyed her parents' order to take her five-year-old sister with her and marry my fourteen-year-old grandfather. This was an old Taiwanese custom: rich families allowed their poor daughter-in-law to bring her younger sister to live with them. Her younger sister would be raised and treated as a non-paid servant in the rich family's house until she got married. My grandmother had never seen my grandfather before she got married. Luckily, my grandfather was wealthy, tall, handsome, and well educated. From the second day after her marriage, my grandmother had to help her mother-in-law with the housework and babysit her own younger sister. She told me that at the beginning, she had to stand on a stool to cook because she was still very short when she got married, but later she grew to one hundred seventy-five centimeters.

The housework was very tedious and difficult for a young woman, but she never complained. Even though she was ridiculed every day by her mother-in-law and father-in-law, and her husband always bossed her, she endured. She said that if a poor girl like her had food to eat, clothes to wear, and a big house to live in, she should feel happy and not complain. Unfortunately, her good life changed after the Japanese were defeated and Taiwan was controlled by China again after World War II.

The new Chinese governor made life miserable for the Taiwanese people; they treated the Taiwanese people badly and unfairly. Eventually, some Taiwanese began to rebel. The Chinese governor tried to stop the rebellion and ordered Chinese soldiers to kill any suspected rebels. This rebellion started on February 28, 1947 and is now known as the 228 Incident. Many students, lawyers, and doctors were killed during this time. Unfortunately, my grandfather's family was among the innocent victims. His elder brother, a famous doctor, was shot, and my grandfather, a pharmacist, was jailed and tortured; he lived, but he was crippled. All the family's property was confiscated. My great-grandfather died a year later and my great-grandmother could not stand the loss of her two sons and became crazy. In addition, my grandmother wanted to protect her two sons from the Chinese soldiers. That was a horrible time for my father's family, but grandmother bravely led the almost broken family safely through this hard time. She told me that she helped her sons hide at Ali Mountain until this incident ended, and she tried her best to comfort her mother-in-law. She also dealt with the terrible Chinese soldiers and begged them to release my grandfather. In addition, she had to go alone to the wild field to collect food and wood fuel for her family every day.

After the incident ended and my grandfather was released from jail, the hard time was still not over. My grandfather had become depressed and addicted to alcohol and smoking. He refused to work and visited brothels every day forgetting his duty to his family. If my grandmother had argued with him, she would have been badly beaten. Even worse, my grandfather decided to take a second wife, a prostitute he met at a brothel. At that time, women had no right to say no to their husband's open unfaithfulness. Strangely, women did have the right to own a business. My grandmother invested in a movie theater and was able to achieve success. So, although my grandmother was very disappointed in her husband, she still worked hard to support the family. She told me that her only comforts at that time were her two sons who successfully attended a famous college and seeing her investment in the movie theater make a profit.

She died of breast cancer at age seventy-four. I was also very impressed with her calm and brave fight with cancer. She always went to the hospital alone for the chemotherapy and radiation treatments and never showed us her anxious and painful feelings. Even in the last moments of her life, she never complained about her indifferent husband, and in her will she left him all her money. Her tremendous courage and great tolerance has inspired me to respect her as a real woman hero, one whose courage I want to emulate.

## Inspiration from My Grandfather

FRANCES WANG

PEOPLE COME INTO THIS WORLD with the possibilities and limitations of when and where they are born. My grandfather on my mother's side was born in China where his future was determined by war and exile. He often cursed his fate and those who started the war. In the 1930's, my grandfather was forced to serve in the Chinese Army because he was young and strong. He left his family and his reluctant mother. The image of her standing at the exit of their village is the last one he has of her. At the end of World War II, China had a civil war and ultimately my grandfather went to Taiwan with the Chinese who were defeated in the Chinese Civil War. Because of the political separation between Taiwan and China, he was not allowed to return to his homeland, even for a visit.

Then, he met my grandmother. During the time between 1950 and 1960, my mother and two aunties were born. Even though they were poor, my grandparents worked extremely hard. My grandfather was working as a policeman in an office every day. My grandmother didn't work outside their home, but she had a home business making things for companies. She made umbrellas or Christmas tree light bulbs. She would send those back to a company to earn money. At times when there was still not enough money, they would sell their valuable things to sustain their family's needs and their children's tuition.

My grandfather lived without his mother's love after he left his village, but he had his own family instead and filled this emptiness. As the time passed, he had been living in Taiwan over half a century. He never visited his homeland, and he never exchanged letters with his mother. Even letters between the two countries were forbidden. Sadly, his mother died before the laws changed to provide access to families to visit one another. He eventually received a letter from one of his relatives telling him of his mother's death. In the letter, his relative described how his mother waited at the front of the village every day of her life. She wanted to be the first one to welcome her son home from the war. When my grandfather read the letter, he was filled with grief and regret. He cried often at the thought of his mother. After many years, my mother and aunties took their father, my grandfather, back to Sichuan, the place where he was born, and they commemorated his mother's life in front her tomb.

I am inspired by this story of my grandfather's life and his love for his family. Even though my grandfather didn't accomplish any extraordinary things, his devotion to his family teaches me an important lesson. My grandfather cherished his family in Taiwan and his mother in China. He could not do something special for his mother. He could not see her or communicate with her. Although he suffered in silence for many years, he was able to love his new family. I never realized how much he loved his mother or how difficult his life was until I heard this story from my mother. From his suffering, I learned to appreciate the time that I have spent with my family, and I appreciate that I was born in a time without war. Before I understood my grandfather's suffering from being separated from his family, I thought that I deserved to leave my family to come to the USA to study. Now, I am studying in the USA, and my family is separated. My father has to work in Taiwan, so he lives there while my mother and my younger brother are here with me.

I feel really grateful every moment that I spend with my family. I feel grateful because, although I miss my father, I can talk to him and communicate with him as often as I want. I am especially grateful to my grandfather for enduring the war years with the ability to love and for showing us how to appreciate family time.

# One Thousand Cranes

### YUKIKO EGAWA

*Senbazuru*, ONE THOUSAND CRANES, ALWAYS reminds me of my grandmother, Toyoko. She was an innovative woman, a lifelong educator, who adored Japanese traditional dance and was a master of Japanese calligraphy. She introduced me to a world outside of Japan and was a model of generosity and kindness.

Several years ago, when I was recently engaged, and my fiancé and I were planning our wedding, we were on top of the world. One morning, my fiancé got a telephone call from Germany that brought frightening news. We learned that his mother, Renate, had had a stroke and was hospitalized. We were shocked. She was only in her late fifties and was in relatively good health. Just a few months earlier, she had visited us and had enjoyed traveling around Japan for three weeks. Fortunately, the stroke was not severe. However, she had to stay in the hospital for several weeks and spend several months in rehabilitation.

When my grandmother, Toyoko, heard about Renate's stroke from my mother, she started to make *senbazuru* for Renate's recovery. *Senbazuru* means one thousand cranes in Japanese. We believe that if we make one thousand origami cranes from special solid colored square paper, our wish will be granted. When our loved ones are seriously sick, we make *origami* cranes as a wish for their recovery. Making one thousand cranes is not so easy. If we don't have really strong perseverance, we won't be able to make them all. If I concentrate, it takes about two minutes to make one crane from a small square of paper. That makes about fifty hours of intense labor to fold one thousand cranes. After the one thousand cranes are folded, they are attached with long strings and hung from the ceiling as one big ornament. It is very colorful and beautiful. It is also a one-of-a-kind precious gift made with love and given with love. If you receive such a gift, you will know that someone cares deeply about you.

My fiancé and I were unaware of my grandmother's thoughtful gesture of friendship and love. She never told us about her commitment to Renate's recovery. We were focused on our wedding plans and concerned about Renate's health. Fortunately, Renate recovered very well, and the stroke left no permanent physical disability. We were all relieved.

The following spring, our wedding was held at one of the oldest shrines in Tokyo. My husband's family came from Germany to attend our wedding and a healthy Renate was with them. After the wedding, Toyoko gave Renate her *senbazuru* to celebrate her healthy recovery. Renate was so touched and appreciated that heartwarming gift. Renate is also a craft lover, so she knew how precious these handcrafted cranes were. The thousand cranes were beautifully connected together with strings and decorated with extra bells. It was about one meter long and thirty centimeters wide. From a distance, the variety of shades and hues made it look like a rainbow waterfall. When it was time to return to Germany after our wedding, Renate carefully packed it and brought it back to Germany, and since then it has been hanging in her living room. My grandmother's *senbazuru* created a strong bond between our Japanese and German families. It was not only a tender gift to Renate. It was also the greatest wedding gift. It is a symbol of her unconditional love for me and demonstrated her support for my marriage. Sadly, this would be her last gift for me.

My grandmother, Toyoko, was born in 1911, the youngest daughter of eight. Since her father was a successful landowner, she was able to get a good education, even though she was a woman. She was rebellious and independent and didn't want to follow the tradition of many women of her day. She envisioned life as a wife and mother in addition to having a professional life. She studied at a university and earned a teaching credential. She married, had six children, and continued to work as a full-time teacher. Actually, she was the source of a steady income for her family. My grandfather, Yoshio, was a dreamer and had political ambitions. He was a candidate for political office several times; however, he was not successful. Toyoko worked as an elementary school teacher for over thirty years. After that, she opened her own pre-kindergarten and worked there as the principal for another twenty years. I have fond memories of playing with my brother in the empty playground on Sunday afternoons when we visited her and grandfather.

My grandmother was a modern woman. As an educator, she traveled to many foreign countries, such as Germany, France, Russia, China and the USA to visit local schools. Her professional life was always important to her. She was modern and daring in other ways as well. At the age of eighty-five, she was still riding a motorbike, a Honda Super Cub. She rode it everywhere in her neighborhood and never relied on others to drive her. She rode it as smoothly and naturally as Lance Armstrong rides his bicycle. When she was wearing her helmet, nobody could guess her age. When her friends called her for help or just to invite her to tea, she hopped on her Super Cub and was ready to go. She also liked to sing and especially liked to sing at karaoke clubs with her friends. With only a glass of iced tea and a microphone in her hand, she was in high spirits. Since she was a warm-hearted woman, so many people loved her. Also, she had a strong will, and if she decided to do something, she always achieved her goal. I respected her and wanted to be like her.

She taught me global thinking through her stories of world travels. She had several unique experiences with local people during her overseas trips. For example, she told me about a time when she and my grandfather were in China. They lost their way and needed help getting back to the hotel. A kind gentleman not only helped them back to the hotel, but he also invited my grandparents to his house for dinner with his family. From her stories, I learned that people are the same all over the world, regardless of race, religion or language. These stories were a stark contrast to the television programs or newspaper articles where I learned only about the difference between Japan and foreign countries. Later, as I traveled to many countries myself, I realized that my grandmother taught me to become friends with people from many countries. Perhaps she was the inspiration for my choice to live outside of Japan and to marry someone from another country. She certainly taught me to appreciate Japanese culture through her practice of calligraphy and Japanese traditional dance. I didn't have to go to a museum to see wonderful art work because I could see them everywhere in her house.

My grandmother's life ended very suddenly. One late summer day, she went to sing *karaoke* at a club with her friends, a usual occurrence. When she got up to sing her song, she held the microphone and stood ready to begin; then she had a heart attack. We were all shocked; however, she died peacefully, doing something she loved.

Now, when I visit my husband's family in Germany, my grandma's *senbazuru* also welcomes us. Every time I see it, I think about Toyoko, how she made it, and how she wished for our happiness, as well as Renate's recovery from her illness. Regretfully, I didn't have a chance to show her directly my appreciation for her dedication to Renate, but she knew how I loved her, and I will always remember how much she loved me. Now I have my own family, and we are all healthy and happy. Even though our family has been living separately, some in Japan, some in Germany, and some in the United States, we are connected in our hearts. I feel my grandmother still protects me from heaven. She also continues to inspire and encourage me to appreciate the world.

## The Memory of My Grandmother
ANONYMOUS

*I* LIKED GOING TO MY GRANDMOTHER'S house during summer and winter vacation when I was in elementary school. I always had a lot of fun even though there were no toys. Grandmother let me play outside in nature and showed me interesting things. She gave me unforgettable memories. She passed away seventeen years ago, yet the memory of her peaceful mind and generous personality continues to be part of my life.

My grandmother lived in a large traditional Korean house in a small country town. This house had both a large vegetable garden with sesame, pepper, squash, eggplant, and other vegetables and a small orchard with apple and plum trees. Sometimes I played with my brother and other children who lived near my grandmother. We played hide-and-seek, caught fish in the stream, and swam in the lake. I also caught frogs and insects like dragonflies or grasshoppers to feed the animals on her farm. She raised many chickens, cows, and pigs. One day she led me to the pigsty to see twelve baby pigs. Another day she gave me a chance to see a calf being born. The moment was so amazing. The calf was wiggling its legs trying to stand up. Soon it started to walk.

My grandmother was a practical and spiritual leader in her family. She had three daughters and six sons. She also lived with her mother-in-law and a nephew who was not married. Her married life began during Japan's occupation of Korea and ended when my grandfather died at the age of forty. He was a leader in his town and was often tortured and beaten by Japanese soldiers for resisting their authority. My grandmother had to become the leader in the family. Fortunately, she didn't have financial difficulties because her family was financially secure. She did, however, have to cope with a hard life by herself. The difficulties of her life never caused her to yell or shout at anyone. She remained generous and kind. For example, if a beggar came to her house for food, which happened often during the occupation and war years, she always offered something.

My grandmother was also a great cook. I especially remember some special treats. During the winter, she gave me sweet *sik-hye*, a traditional Korean rice juice, or an acorn jelly salad. My favorite was a cold bean noodle soup. It had a bundle of thin wheat noodles in a thick salty broth made from ground beans. It was perfect during the hot, humid summer nights. I always felt comfortable in her presence even when my parents were not there.

I am fast approaching the age she was when I spent so much time with her. I am not, however, as kind or generous, nor is my cooking as good. My sons wish I cooked as well for them as she did for me. Now I realize what a great woman she was, and she has become my role model. I have frequently heard my relatives say that she and my mom had much in common in mind and personality. I want to claim this precious inheritance from my grandmother through my mom. I hope I will be like them someday!

## A Journey Too Short
ANONYMOUS

THE LIFE OF MY SISTER Gaby was not easy, yet she was determined and persistent in pursuing her happiness and overcoming difficult circumstances. Gaby was the oldest of seven children and brought hope, joy, and love into our dysfunctional family, where the lack of love, patience, and care from our parents were our daily bread. However, at an early age, she understood that our father's addiction to alcohol and our mother's neurosis were the result of their unhappiness and frustrations. She was determined not to continue the destructive pattern of our parents and their parents, but to pursue her own path. Gaby learned to live within the chaos but never surrendered to it. For instance, when our father came home drunk, she would already have finished her homework, her first priority, and she would help our mother with the household chores. As soon as our parents' arguments started, she would take us, me and all our brothers and sisters, to the park or to a place where we could study, do crafts, or tell stories. She tried to distract us so we would not experience the unhealthy environment.

Gaby was always a diligent student with her eye on the future and with an understanding that she would find refuge for herself and others through her education. At the age of twenty-two, she graduated from the university with a degree in social services. Despite our parents' opposition and poverty, she achieved her first goal. Throughout her education, in the face of our parents' constant confrontations, she worked double shifts and studied at the same time.

After she achieved her educational goals and began her career, she never forgot her roots. She continued her journey, helping not only her family and friends, but also helping people in need. She especially enjoyed working with senior citizens and giving them and her coworkers love, advice, and friendship.

Gaby's short life of taking care of and inspiring others came to an abrupt end. Three months before her twenty-eighth birthday, she was diagnosed with cervical cancer. In less than a month, the cancer had spread to all her major organs. She died quickly and without pain. Our family was devastated as were all the people who knew her. Her funeral, the celebration of her short life, was a testament to the influence she had on the world. Her family, friends, and coworkers gathered in agreement about how lovely Gaby was and about how she loved and enjoyed life. After the funeral, the procession to the cemetery included three buses and many cars all packed with senior citizens, coworkers, friends and family who accompanied Gaby. At the funeral, I felt like I was going to have a heart attack, but at the same time, my heart was comforted by all the people who came to say good-bye and to express their affection for Gaby. My eyes filled with bitter tears and my heart saddened at the loss of my beloved sister. I also understood that love brings peace and happiness.

Gaby lived her life fully, with generosity and kindness even in the face of hardship. She motivated me to follow her example, and when I feel frustrated or want to quit, I think of her. Her life gives me the courage and determination to pursue my happiness.

# My Father

MARIA ELENA URZUA

*A*FTER I GREW UP, I realized that my father was a very important person in my life. When I was little, sometimes I felt that he was very strict and serious. As a teenager, I believed that he was no fun, and sometimes I thought he was even a bad dad. Eventually, I learned to appreciate and respect my dad's extraordinary character.

My father had a very rough childhood. When he was just five years old, his mother died, leaving his father with four young children. His father, unprepared for the task of raising his children, abandoned them. He left them in the care of his sisters who took them in but couldn't create a loving environment. By the time my father was a teenager, nobody took care of him any longer. At an age when most children are still under the watchful eye of their parents as they approach adulthood, he got a job and accepted responsibility for himself. His childhood was lost when his mother died, yet he made his own way in the world and eventually gave his own children the childhood he never had.

My father accepted his role as a parent with great responsiblity. He worked hard to provide his children with everything they wanted and needed. He worked in the same office for the same company throughout his career. He could have retired when he was only fifty years old, but he continued working so that he could live his dreams and take care of his family. For example, as my parents started to have children, my father wanted a house so he bought a lot and built a house. As more children came, he decided to have a bigger house in a better neighborhood.

My father understood how important it was for children to have interesting experiences and fond memories of their childhood. He made sure that we did a lot of interesting things with our family. He liked camping and traveling, so I spent all my vacations camping throughout Mexico and even in the USA. We camped all around my country, from south to north, from west to east. We visited many archeological sites like Chichen Itza, Monte Alban, Tajin, and Teotihuacan. He bought a camper and planned all our trips with great detail. We all helped to set up the camp, cook the meals, and wash the dishes. Every trip we had a wonderful time. My father also wanted us to have a vacation home, so he bought a house in the countryside in Contepec, where we spent many weekends. I loved to go there. It was my father's hometown, so when we were there, he was relaxed and encouraged us to explore and have fun. As a result of my father's love of travel, I have a passion to see new places. I think traveling was one of the best gifts my father could have given me.

My dad was exceptional as a parent. He had modern ideas about raising children, perhaps because his childhood allowed him to trust his judgment and ours. Compared to my friends' experience, we had few rules. Mexico is very traditional regarding daughters leaving home before marriage, but my dad never followed those cultural expectations. He never made us follow traditions; instead, he encouraged us to be independent and to make our own decisions. Some of my friends' dads never let them go out; my father let me do many things. I had permission to go out and travel with friends, but I knew I had to study hard and make responsible decisions.

He showed us through example how to take responsibility for ourselves. My dad was a great planner. He always had everything very well thought-out and well prepared. He saved money for the future but made sure we could enjoy the present. He invested in property to ensure our security throughout his life and ours. He even chose the cemetery and the coffins we would be buried in.

My father also understood that we needed to be prepared for successful lives. I admire him because even though he didn't have a college education, he encouraged us to earn a degree. He always knew that having an education would help us to have good jobs. My father encouraged us to go to school and be responsible, not missing classes even if we were sick. We needed to be almost dying before we could miss school. Now, each of my three sisters, my brother, and I have university degrees.

My father taught us to be honest and loyal and to respect the law. He never even got a traffic ticket; he always followed the rules. He taught us to always tell the truth and be responsible for our actions. I am very proud of my dad and the work he did with us. Unfortunately, he passed away several years ago, but he is with me every moment of my life. He influences the way I live my life and the way I raise my own children. My children know all about their wonderful grandpa. I love my father and appreciate everything he contributed to my life.

## Eulogy
MARILYN MARQUIS

WHEN I TOLD MY COUSIN David that my mother had died, he sighed and exclaimed, "She was a spectacular woman!" Indeed she was. She was remarkable in her devotion, tolerance, and independence. She welcomed friendship from people of all walks of life, of all ages and experiences, and yet, never waivered in her traditional beliefs and practices. She practiced her religion with devotion; she enjoyed attending mass every week and found great solace in daily prayer, yet she never required her children or grandchildren to embrace her religious practice. In spite of her religious dedication, she quietly supported political views that were not supported by her church. In many ways, I did not fully understand her until the end of her life. When I heard from her nieces and nephews, her grandchildren, and her friends, I understood how truly extraordinary she was.

I have always enjoyed telling students about my family, especially my mother's immigrant family. Many of my students expressed surprise that my mother lived alone when she was over ninety years old. In many cultures, older people want to live with one of their children. Not my mother. She was always fiercely independent and enjoyed making her own decisions and taking care of herself. Of course, she enjoyed visiting us and our visiting her, but she never wanted to be a burden to anyone, nor did she want to give up her independence. She enjoyed her friends in the Italian Catholic Federation. These good friends went to church together, played poker regularly, attended luncheons and dinners, went shopping, and generally had lots of fun together. She kept herself busy and satisfied throughout her life.

She was also an independent thinker. After her death, when I was looking through her things, I found this prayer.

*Until every person lives in dignity, none of us can live in peace. O God our loving father, you sent your son Jesus to bring us, your people, fullness of life. Free all those who suffer because of sickness, injustice, oppression, or fear, and unite us all in your kingdom now and in eternity. Amen*

This prayer helped me to understand my mother and realize why she was a spectacular woman. She rarely expressed her opinions in conversation, but she did express them through her actions in support of those who suffer. She worked to bring that dignity to all.

For example, in the early 1960's, when I was in high school, my mother volunteered at the Camarillo State Hospital where she was a special friend to Maureen, a young girl with serious mental illness. She visited her every week for several years and on occasion invited Maureen to spend weekends with our family. We learned to appreciate Maureen by spending time with her and discovering that her strange behavior should not frighten us or be reason to reject her. My brothers and sister and I developed great affection for Maureen and learned to appreciate the gifts of those who are different from us. My mother continued her friendship with Maureen and her family for many years.

And at the end of her life, my mother chose to donate all of her worldly goods to the Desert AIDS Project in the hope that her donation would help free those who suffer from that terrible disease. She also understood that this gesture expressed her commitment to promoting the dignity of all. This was a surprise to her sisters and especially to her friends in the Italian Catholic Federation. The church has long rejected homosexuality as sinful, a view my mother never shared. This generosity of spirit and expression of dignity for all made me feel very proud. She had the rare ability to treat everyone with respect, fairness, and dignity, which stems from her belief in the dignity of all humanity.

She was also a spectacular mother, and my brothers, sister and I benefited greatly from her wisdom and her ability to not say too much. She respected our dignity, allowed us the freedom to make mistakes, and never belabored them.

She could forgive and forget and would never punish too severely for youthful indiscretions. She gave us the freedom to be ourselves and taught us that we are responsible for the decisions we make. We knew, however, that she would be there to help with the consequences. She continued to be a supportive force in our lives. Long after we became parents ourselves, she made us our favorite cookies, surprised us with gifts she thought we might like, listened to our concerns, helped us cope with our struggles, and shared our joys. We were indeed most fortunate to be hers.

She embraced her life. At the end of her life, she also embraced her death. She had lived a long and interesting earthly life and was ready for the next.

She learned, however, that the end of life would not be as swift and easy as she had hoped. Her dignity was challenged by her sudden illness. She had to rely on others, who like herself, believed that every person should live in dignity. Hope Hospice brought her new friends and opened her heart and mind to new ideas, conversations unlike any she had ever had, and awareness that she could accept help.

She left this world grateful for her wonderful life. No one could ask for more.

# Using *One World Many Voices*

Both intensive and extensive reading are important aspects of an ESL reading curriculum. The essays in *One World Many Voices* are designed to provide interesting and easy extensive reading material. They can, however, be used effectively in many ways in the classroom. While extensive reading contributes to overall language proficiency growth and helps students to become successful readers, intensive reading provides instructor-led activities that help students develop reading proficiency and confidence.

Teachers can address factors that lead to unsuccessful and successful reading in the classroom through both intensive and extensive reading activities. Extensive reading alone will not remedy unsuccessful reading practices, but a combination of extensive reading and teacher-led intensive reading activities will remedy most.

## FACTORS IN SUCCESSFUL AND UNSUCCESSFUL READING

### Factors in Unsuccessful Reading

- Lack of rapid, automatic, and accurate word recognition
- Limited sight vocabulary
- Lack of phonological competence
- Limited grasp of the structure of the language
- Inability to disambiguate information in the text
- Inability to use reading strategies flexibly while reading
- Lack of general world knowledge
- Lack of interaction between textual and general world knowledge
- Rigidity in perception and conceptualization

## Factors in Successful Reading

- Rapid, automatic, and accurate word recognition
- Large recognition vocabulary
- Reasonable grasp of the structure of the language
- Ability to disambiguate information
- Ability to establish a standard of coherence, monitor comprehension, set goals, and use strategies to reach that standard
- Ability to integrate meaning
- Ability to make inferences and connections to background knowledge
- Ability to suppress less important information
- Fluency in processing words, sentences, and discourse cues

### EXTENSIVE READING

Extensive reading can help second language readers overcome some factors that lead to unsuccessful reading. Guided extensive reading programs provide readers with carefully selected material and suggestions for reading frequency. They promote reading fluency much the way that journal writing helps students become fluid writers. Most significantly, extensive reading provides reading practice. It guides time-on-task for readers who might not be self-motivated.

### Material

In order to promote fluency, extensive reading material should be easy to read with few unfamiliar words and easy-to-process sentence structure. Students should be able to read faster than they read for intensive reading and should be encouraged not to use a dictionary. The purpose of extensive reading is general understanding.

The essays in these collections are carefully edited for different proficiency levels of English learners. The vocabulary increases in breadth from the most frequent 500 words to the most frequent 2,000 words in English across the series. The sentence structure also increases in complexity over the collections.

The essays in *Reflections* were edited for sentence structure and vocabulary to provide advanced level students with interesting and easy to read extensive reading material.

Each book in the series can provide a portion of the required extensive reading material for one semester. At every level of proficiency, students should engage in extensive reading four to five times a week in addition to the reading they do in class.

## The Teacher's Role

Teachers can encourage, inspire, and motivate students to read by engaging in extensive reading along with their students in the classroom and by establishing an expectation of extensive reading outside of the classroom. Teachers are excellent models for reading and discussing books. They can share their own experiences with reading and tell students about the books they are reading. When teachers read the same books that the students are reading, they can share their reactions to the books and guide student discussions. Language learners often have limited experience reading in English or discussing things they read in their new language. The teacher can model these activities and encourage students to discuss their reading with each other.

Teachers might introduce extensive reading with activities that invite students to examine their reading experiences, habits, and attitudes toward reading in their first language.

### Goals of Extensive Reading

Extensive reading can help second language readers overcome some factors that lead to unsuccessful reading practices. The goals of extensive reading include the following:

- Improve reading comprehension
- Increase rapid, automatic, and accurate recognition of the most frequent English words
- Encourage incidental vocabulary learning
- Increase reading rate
- Gain overall language proficiency
- Build general knowledge
- Support the development of a reader identity in English
- Establish a community of readers

## Suggestions for Teacher Directed Activities

The essays in *Reflections* can be used as a classroom resource not only for extensive reading practice, but also for achieving overall reading goals. They are a resource for practicing reading skills and strategies that promote successful reading. The following suggestions have emerged from our experience using the essays in the classroom. We hope that you find them useful.

### IMPROVE COMPREHENSION

Book discussions can help language learners develop a sense of competence and autonomy as they read for comprehension. Discussion activities can help them monitor their comprehension and motivate them to develop comprehension strategies. Such strategies include re-reading, looking for key words or ideas, constructing mental summaries, and connecting ideas encountered in the text to their own experiences. Here are some activities that can help learners improve their comprehension.

· After reading a passage once, tell a partner about the passage without looking at the text.

· Read a passage multiple times and tell a partner about the passage without looking at the text. Discuss the comprehension differences after a third or fourth reading.

· Connect the ideas in an essay to personal experience.

· Identify the most important ideas in an essay.

· In pairs or small groups, discuss an essay in light of similarities and/or differences with personal experience.

## LEARN AND PRACTICE READING STRATEGIES

Students learn reading strategies from their reading textbooks and practice applying those strategies during teacher-guided activities in class. The essays in this book can provide additional practice opportunities for mastering those strategies and for supporting their integration into students' independent reading practices. Here are some activities that can provide learners with opportunities to practice various reading strategies.

· Ask students to preview the book and discuss its overall organization as a class.

· After reading a chapter, ask students to work in pairs or small groups to draw inferences about one or more of the essays. For example, students might be asked to draw inferences about cultural expectations or values not explicitly discussed in an essay.

· Ask students to discuss their previous knowledge or experience with a topic from one of the chapters. For example, ask students to tell about celebrating important events.

· Ask students to scan for particular information. For example, students might scan a passage for key words or ideas.

· Select one essay in a chapter and ask students to look for transitions signals, key words, or other coherence devices that link ideas within and between paragraphs.

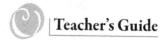 

## INCREASE READING RATE

Slow readers spend a great deal of time processing individual letters and words, making it difficult for them to understand what they are reading. Reading faster will aid comprehension and increase reading pleasure. It will also contribute to overall academic success. English language learners will naturally increase their reading speed over time as their general language proficiency increases, but with practice and guidance their reading speed can increase more quickly. Here are some activities that can help students increase their reading speed.

### Reading Pairs

1. Select a passage from the book. Ask students to work with a partner.
2. Partner A reads aloud for 30 seconds.
3. Partner B reads the same passage for 30 seconds.
4. Repeat.
5. Ask how many more words were read each time.

### Reading Sprints

1. Select a passage from the book. Ask students to read silently for four minutes. Use a timer or a watch with a second hand. Then ask them to count the number of lines they read.
2. Students then count out the same number of lines in the next part of the passage. They continue reading for three minutes, trying to read the same number of lines in less time. Students count the lines they read in three minutes, count out the same number of lines in the next part of the passage, and try to read as many lines in two minutes.
3. When the reading sprint is complete, the class can discuss their comprehension of the text.

### Monitor

1. Encourage students to monitor their reading speed.
2. Have students chart their progress.

RAPID, ACCURATE, AUTOMATIC WORD RECOGNITION

Increased reading comprehension and reading speed are only possible when students can rapidly and accurately recognize large numbers of words in print. Their vocabulary for listening and speaking is not accessed for reading unless they also recognize what a word looks like on the printed page and then connect that word to their mental lexicon. Extensive reading exposes language learners to the printed word, but it does not ensure that students accurately process the correct meaning. Some read aloud activities can help language learners connect printed words to the vocabulary they have developed for listening and speaking. It can also provide consistent pronunciation practice.

### Read Aloud

- After students read a passage silently twice, ask them to read it aloud to a partner.
- Assign one paragraph of a passage to each student. For homework the student should practice reading aloud, focusing on careful pronunciation and phrasing. In class, students read to each other.

### Pronunciation

- Encourage students to use the computer software or Internet interface of an English language learner dictionary and ensure that students know the pronunciation of the a large number of the most frequent English words.
- Encourage students to say and write words to promote the connection between the written and spoken forms.
- Make pronunciation an important part of knowing a word.

## ENCOURAGE INCIDENTAL LEARNING AND DEEPEN WORD KNOWLEDGE

Sometimes students believe that reading will help their vocabulary development only if reading texts contain many new words. Talking to students about the value of reading easy texts for learning vocabulary may help them see the value of extensive reading more clearly.

Extensive reading can also help students deepen their knowledge of known words since knowing a word includes many types of knowledge such as knowing the spelling, pronunciation, and multiple meanings of the word. Simple activities such as reading aloud, listening and repeating, and listening to audio files of passages can all contribute to deepening learners' knowledge of a word. Teachers can also direct students' attention to words in a passage that draw on less frequent uses of those words.

## LINK READING AND WRITING

Regular journal writing about topics from their reading can promote both reading and writing fluency. Ungraded reflective writing about their ideas after reading promotes close reading, encourages readers to explore reactions to the text, gives them a chance to examine features of a text more closely, and encourages readers to link their own experiences to those of the writer. Here are some possible journal prompts.

- What does the author mean by...?
- How are the experiences of the authors different from or similar to your experiences?
- What did you think about as you read...?
- What was interesting/confusing about this essay/chapter?
- Write about an important tradition in your culture.

## INCREASE OVERALL LANGUAGE PROFICIENCY

Listening, speaking, reading, and writing in English all require knowledge of grammar. Reading easy and interesting material, as students do with extensive reading, helps them confirm their knowledge of English grammar and provides extensive input upon which to make further generalizations about English grammar. Here are some activity types that can help learners gain overall language proficiency.

### Sound-Spelling Relationship

- A student whose native language uses a writing system that is very different from the English alphabet will likely benefit from activities that focus attention on sound-spelling relationships.
- Copying a paragraph can give students easy practice with forming letters and spelling.

### Grammar Analysis

Analyzing the grammar in a passage helps students to focus on language structure and to discuss their observations. Each activity should take no more than 15 minutes. The possibilities are endless, but here are some ideas.

1. First, select a paragraph that has a sufficient number of the target structure and make an overhead transparency of the paragraph.

2. Students should first work alone for three minutes to identify as many examples of the target structure as they can.

3. Next, ask students to work in pairs to confirm their findings.

4. Finally show your own findings on the overhead. At the advanced level, students benefit from identifying the subject and verb in each clause. They can identify noun phrases, prepositional phrases, subject phrases, and verb phrases. They can find pronouns and referents, gerund and infinitive phrases. They can analyze the punctuation, and they can also make generalizations about articles by observing them in the text.

## DEVELOP FLUENCY

Reading fluency and speaking fluency often develop at different rates. When students have opportunities to talk about what they are reading, they bring together multiple skills. The activities below also encourage integrating reading and speaking skills as well as multiple readings of a text, which can deepen understanding and enable readers to see something new with each reading.

### Read Aloud

Students should read a passage silently multiple times and rehearse before reading it aloud to a partner.

### Oral Summaries

Students retell passages from memory and confirm comprehension.

1. Students read one entry as many times as they can for 10–12 minutes.
2. With a partner, retell/summarize the passage.
3. Identify key points with the whole class.
4. Read the passage again.

### Summary Sprints

In pairs, students summarize a passage.

1. Student A has three minutes to summarize the passage.
2. Student B has two minutes to summarize the same passage.
3. Student A has one minute to summarize the same passage.

## BUILD GENERAL KNOWLEDGE

Each chapter in *Reflections* focuses on personal experience. Most also include information about the writer's culture or experience with American culture. This diversity of experiences provides geographical, cultural, religious, and family perspectives and provides an opportunity for readers to develop knowledge about cultures and countries very different from their own. They can confirm their new knowledge through discussion activities or research assignments.

## ENGAGE IN CRITICAL THINKING

Students need practice thinking and analyzing as they read. Some simple activities that encourage students to think about organization of ideas and how ideas relate across several essays can help students to do this on their own. Here are some examples of how to use the book to encourage critical thinking.

- Each chapter in the book reflects on a particular aspect of the human life cycle. Select several passages about the same type of experience, and ask students to work in small groups to identify some similarities.
- Encourage students to draw conclusions from reading about a particular type of celebration. Ask critical thinking questions such as why a particular celebration was important to the author, what aspects of the celebration reveals something about the author's culture, or what the author does not express that might be important.
- Ask students to select their favorite essay from a given chapter and to tell a group of students the reasons for their opinions.

## SUPPORT READER IDENTITY IN ENGLISH

Developing an identity as an English reader over the course of several semesters can help language learners transition from learning to read to reading to learn. Extensive reading provides the time on task that builds confidence, promotes learning, and provides practice. All of which can lead to increased pleasure reading, other types of independent reading, and related oral or written activities that readers engage in as part of what it means to be a reader. Activities that invite students to discuss or write about their experiences as English readers can help them be more aware of their development of an English reader identity.

## CREATE A COMMUNITY OF READERS

Many of us have had the pleasurable experience of talking to friends and colleagues about a book we have read. When we discuss our own reading with others, we become part of a larger community of readers. When language learners engage in reading the same book as part of their extensive reading, they have the opportunity to experience that same pleasure. They share their ideas and participate in a community that values reading and sharing ideas about that reading.

# Countries

AFGHANISTAN
BRAZIL
CAMBODIA
CHINA
CUBA
ETHIOPIA
GERMANY
GHANA
INDIA
INDONESIA
IRAN
JAPAN
KOREA
MEXICO
NIGERIA
PHILIPPINES
POLAND
RUSSIA
SERBIA
TAIWAN
THAILAND
UKRAINE
USA

# Index of Authors

*M*ARILYN MARQUIS TEACHES ESL AT Las Positas College in Livermore, California. She was inspired to become an ESL teacher after hosting two young people through the Experiment in International Living. She began teaching English as a Second Language at Long Beach City College in 1983 and was an adjunct English and ESL teacher there until 1991 when she joined the faculty at Las Positas College. Reading instruction has been an area of particular interest to her throughout her professional life. She has enjoyed the collaboration on this series of student-generated essays. Marilyn holds a bachelor's degree in English from California State University, Northridge and a master's degree from California State University, Dominguez Hills.

*S*ARAH NIELSEN HAS BEEN INTERESTED in language learning and teaching since she was a high school student. She spent a year in Belgium living with a French-speaking family and attending school before she began her university education. She taught English in China for two years before entering graduate school. She began teaching as an adjunct ESL instructor in 1995 before joining the faculty at Las Positas College in 2000. In 2004, she joined the faculty at California State University, East Bay, as the coordinator of the MA TESOL program. Sarah holds a bachelor's degree from the University of California, Santa Cruz, and both a master's degree, and a Ph.D. from the University of California, Davis.

CPSIA information can be obtained
at www.ICGtesting.com
Printed in the USA
FSHW010909130821
83880FS